CONTENTS

CONTENTS

CONTENTS

CONTENTS

AUTHORS' INDEX

ACKNOWLEDGEMENTS

FOR permission to reprint copyright material in this anthology the compilers and publishers are grateful to the following authors, author's representatives, and publishers:

Jean Anouilh: the Author's representative Dr Jan van Loewen

Enid Bagnold: the Author

J. M. Barrie: Michael and Simon Asquith

Anton Chekhov: Elisaveta Fen and Penguin Books Ltd

Warren Chetham-Strode: the Author

Shelagh Delaney: the Author and Methuen & Co. Ltd

R. F. Delderfield: the Author

Jennette Dowling and Francis Letton: the Authors

Daphne du Maurier: the Author

Christopher Fry: the Author and Oxford University Press

Carlo Goldoni: (from *The Servant of Two Masters*) Edward J. Dent and Cambridge University Press and (from *The Fan*) Oxford University Press

Ronald Gow: the Author

Graham Greene: the Author and Heinemann Educational Books Ltd

William Douglas Home: the Author and Evans Plays

Henrik Ibsen: the Translator and Penguin Books Ltd

Saunders Lewis: the Author, the Translator and Elek Books Ltd

Carson McCullers: the Author and Ashley Famous Agency Inc.

T. B. Morris: the Author

John Osborne: the Author and Faber and Faber Ltd

James Saunders: the Author and Heinemann Educational Books Ltd

Peter Shaffer: the Author

George Bernard Shaw: the Public Trustee and The Society of Authors

N. F. Simpson: the Author

Dodie Smith: the Author

Sophocles: the Translator and John Murray (Publishers) Ltd

Joan Temple: the Author and Sampson Low, Marston and Co Ltd

Ivan Turgenev: Emlyn Williams and Heinemann Educational Books Ltd

John van Druten: A. D. Peters and Co

Arnold Wesker: the Author and Jonathan Cape Ltd

Emlyn Williams: the Author and Heinemann Educational Books Ltd

Tennessee Williams: the Author

ACKNOWLEDGMENTS

The author wishes to express his grateful thanks to this anthology, the compilers and publishers. Grateful thanks to the following authors and publishers, dramatists, and publishers.

INTRODUCTION

WE called the first book of *Scenes for Two* "Duologues for Young Players" as it comprised extracts suitable for girls and boys of fifteen years or under. Book II cannot be so specifically classified. Most people over the age of fifteen wish to work on adult material, and it was with this in mind that we made our choices for this volume.

Wanting a comprehensive term to describe all females over fifteen years old, we found ourselves stuck for a sub-title. A dip into Roget's Thesaurus yielded "wenches", "nanny-goats" and "nymphs" among other choice epithets, so we gave up and decided not to try to be original, but to call Book II precisely what it is, "a book of duologues for girls and women".

This will mean that the book's usefulness should not be confined to secondary schools, but that it should also be valuable to drama school students, youth clubs, and drama groups, as well as organizations for older women. Our selections include extracts from English and foreign literature; from old and new plays, and from tragedies and comedies. They provide an opportunity for acting in many styles, and for developing character work. We have not included any extracts for men or boys, as we feel there is not the same need; finding material for two men, or one girl and one man, is not a problem.

As in our previous book, we would point out that though the synopses explain the plot and characters up to the beginning of the scene, it is always more rewarding to read the play as a whole.

"AND NO BIRDS SING"

By Jenny Laird and John Fernald

Elizabeth Payling, a clever, poised, successful doctor, is revered by her twenty-year-old ward, whom she rescued from poverty. Paulie, though herself attractive and intelligent, has an inferiority complex, and feeling that her doctor boy friend does not love her, becomes ill.

Scene—*Dr Elizabeth Payling's house, London.*
Time—*1946.*

ELIZABETH. Sit down, Paulie; I want to talk to you. (*Her tone is not too sympathetic*)

(PAULIE *crosses down* C *and sits in the armchair.* ELIZABETH *moves towards her slightly*)

(*She chooses her words with care*) You're a silly little ass, aren't you? (*She points at the grapes*) Look, George brought you those.

(PAULIE *glances at them indifferently. There is a slight pause*)

On the fifteenth of March, four years ago, you sat on the edge of the pavement telling stories to a little boy called Tommy Moore, shortly before he died. Do you remember?

(PAULIE *nods*)

When I looked at you then I thought you were one of the bravest people I'd ever seen. When I look at you now I think I must have been wrong.

(PAULIE *looks uneasy.* ELIZABETH *changes her position*)

I was trying to imagine the other day how it would feel to open the door of my life and walk out. Whether it would be dark or light outside, whether I should still be me—or nothing; a smudge, a ghost, a memory. Wouldn't it be interesting to know?

(PAULIE'S *uneasiness increases.* ELIZABETH *comes down to Paulie's* R)

I wonder if a suicide wishes he could turn back when it's too late? It must be a ghastly moment when he realizes just what he's done. Something snaps in his brain and he sees clearly again—all the little things he has despised or forgotten—firelight—rain—clowns at the circus—a day at the zoo with all those vulgar monkeys. . . . I should think the most fantastic things swim through one's head, wouldn't you? (*She moves to the back of Paulie's chair*) You're feeling

I

pretty hopeless, aren't you? Well, I'll tell you something, Paulie. There's something that's more important than hope, and that's courage. Courage to face the loneliness of living. All your life you'll be alone. Everybody is, so why expect anything else? Alone from the minute you're hauled into the world. Then afterwards alone in all your most important moments; your pleasure, your pain, your little private hell. And most alone of all when you die. How very lonely that solitary exit must be. While Ken holds another girl in his arms and says, "Och, you're bonny!" (*She moves away to the stairs*)

PAULIE. He doesn't say "Och!"

ELIZABETH (*ignoring her*) But of course, it's up to you. Only there are certain experiences it's a pity to have missed. One of them is marriage. There's nothing in the world as comic as marriage, especially when your husband starts telling you how to bring up the baby. But perhaps you wouldn't see that—you're too damn self-centred to have a sense of humour.

PAULIE. That's a lie!

ELIZABETH (*with deliberate brutality*) Well, aren't you? Can't you see what an ass you're making of yourself right now? All you want is to lie on a bier in white nightdress holding a lily, with everybody shedding tears around you and saying how sad. You little phoney.

PAULIE. Shut up!

ELIZABETH. Then what are you doing with that bottle in your pocket? Come on—give it to me.

(PAULIE *hesitates, takes it from her pocket, puts it on the table, and rises. She crosses quickly to the settee where she sits down at the* R *end, with her back turned.* ELIZABETH *crosses to the round table, examines the bottle, and finds to her relief that it is nearly full. She looks at Paulie pityingly and moves to her, but continues to speak in a hard voice*)

Well? What did you think Ken was going to say when he saw you being violently sick? You wouldn't die, you know, you'd just be sick, I should see to that.

(PAULIE, *completely deflated, leans her head on her hands*)

PAULIE (*hardly audibly*) You are a cow. . . .

(ELIZABETH *smiles, but then deliberately reassumes her expression of severity*)

ELIZABETH. When did you take that bottle out of my bag?

PAULIE (*half tearfully*) I don't know—two days ago . . .

ELIZABETH. And ever since you've been making up your mind whether to live or die. I suppose I ought to be sorry for you, but I never did go for histrionics.

PAULIE. Liz . . .

ELIZABETH. Romantic death, my foot! You'll live to be ninety and all your teeth will drop out. . . .

(PAULIE *rises towards her, half-laughing, half-tearful*)

Don't come crying to me. If I were you I should go into the dining-room and see if Ken's not too bored to take you back—I should think he probably is.

PAULIE (*furious*) That's where you're wrong—you know nothing about men!

ELIZABETH. Well, I know that they like a woman to be a woman —not a spoilt self-centred baby with an exhibitionist complex!

(PAULIE *slaps Elizabeth's face.* ELIZABETH *gives a laugh of triumph*)

That's better!

(*For a second* PAULIE *stands petrified. Then she collapses into the settee and bursts into tears.* ELIZABETH *relaxes, sits beside her, and gently kisses her. From now on she allows herself her normal, friendly manner, although underneath she is very highly emotional*)

Listen, Monkey, what you need is a life of your own. You've been trying to live through me, and so *you've* ceased to exist. I was a fool not to see it before, and I shan't forgive myself.

PAULIE. It wasn't you . . .

ELIZABETH. Yes, it was. You're not a tough old careerist like me, and I shouldn't have let you think it. Your future's standing there in the dining-room drinking bottled beer, and I think you ought to stop him going on to the whisky!

ELIZABETH *pulls Paulie up with a gesture towards the dining-room door. Paulie still hesitates in the centre of the room.*
ELIZABETH *crosses to the door down* R *and calls.*

Doctor Tweedie! Over to you.

ANN VERONICA

By RONALD GOW

From the book by H. G. WELLS

Ann, twenty-two, of upper-middle-class family, leaves home to fight for emancipation with the Suffragette Movement. Having lived in poverty and endured prison, she returns home, intending to marry Hubert Manning, the worshipping young man, who has been her friend for many years, but whom she does not love.

SCENE—*The garden at Morningside Park.*
TIME—*1909.*

MISS STANLEY. Oh, there you are, Ann Veronica. I've had a note from Lady Palsworthy. She suggests a marquee in the garden. She says the house is too small to accommodate the guests. What do you think about a marquee?

ANN (*shrugging her shoulders*) It makes it sound like a cattle show.

MISS STANLEY. That's all, Maggie, thank you.

(MAGGIE *exits* R. *The soft, distant music of a piano is heard—possibly Chopin's Nocturne No. 2, Opus 9*)

What did your father say, dear, about the wedding dress?

ANN (*moving above and slightly* L *of the table*) I can have it.

MISS STANLEY. Oh, I'm glad. (*She continues to play patience*) Ann Veronica. I want you to have great happiness.

(ANN *looks up at the sky*)

It's something I never really had myself, but I've seen it coming to other women and I hope it's coming to you. (*She notices* ANN *looking upwards*) What are you looking at over there?

ANN. Only the stars.

MISS STANLEY. Very appropriate. And how romantic. I know these days go very slowly for you, my dear—but remember I shall still be sitting here, when you've gone, with my patience cards—and thinking about you.

ANN. Someone's playing a piano—a long way off.

MISS STANLEY. Yes, dear, I think I can hear it. There, I don't want to listen. (*She shivers*) I think music in a garden at night is so sad. (*She surveys the cards*) Oh, dear, I don't think this is going to come out.

ANN. Aunt Molly.

4

MISS STANLEY. Yes, dear.

ANN. Will you tell me something, Aunty?

MISS STANLEY. Yes, my dear. What is it?

ANN. Were you ever in love?

MISS STANLEY (*sitting back*) Gracious! (*She attends to her game*) What makes you ask that?

ANN. I wondered. You've never told me anything.

(MISS STANLEY *moves another card*)

Were you?

MISS STANLEY (*after a slight pause; gently*) We were engaged for seven years. Then he died.

ANN (*gently*) I see. I'm terribly sorry.

MISS STANLEY. It would have been very rash and unwise anyway.

ANN. Why?

MISS STANLEY. His stipend was altogether insufficient to keep us both. You see—I had no money of my own.

ANN. And you really loved him?

MISS STANLEY. Of course, my dear . . .

ANN. Are you sorry you waited?

MISS STANLEY. One must wait. Life is like that for a woman. Then your mother died, and your father invited me to Morningside Park. I've been here ever since. And of course I'm very grateful.

ANN. The wrappered life!

MISS STANLEY (*looking up at Ann*) I beg your pardon?

ANN. The wrappered life—in Morningside Park. Like being wrapped in layers and layers of cotton-wool. (*She moves a pace or two away* L)

MISS STANLEY. I don't know what you mean.

ANN (*turning, and easing towards the table*) Aunt Molly, don't you ever feel that you and I had ancestors who swung by their heels from trees and did dreadful things?

MISS STANLEY. Certainly not. I'm sure I never had ancestors like that.

ANN (*pointing to a card*) You can put the ten on the jack.

MISS STANLEY. So I can.

ANN. Tell me more about the man you loved.

MISS STANLEY. He was of very good family. He was a curate. We were to be married when he got a living.

ANN. Suppose you had married him without waiting.

MISS STANLEY. I've told you. We had nothing.

ANN. I said—suppose you had married him.

MISS STANLEY. I might have ruined his career.

ANN. You'd have lived in a garret?

MISS STANLEY. Somewhere dreadful.

ANN. Your little world would have turned against you.

MISS STANLEY. Oh yes—indeed it would.

ANN. You'd have defied everybody.

MISS STANLEY (*unconsciously impulsive*) Yes! (*She recollects herself*)
Why do you say that? I remember one night when he came to see
me—and he wanted to do that . . .

ANN (*eagerly*) Then you'd have won, you'd have conquered—
you'd have had him.

MISS STANLEY (*exultant*) Yes! I'd have had him! (*She checks herself*)
Oh, no . . . What are you making me say? Ann Veronica, I don't
like you saying these things. It's most unsettling. (*She rings the little
bell on her table*)

ANN. I'm sorry. Please forget what I said.

MISS STANLEY. I must go in now. (*She rises*) It's getting cold.
(*Moving to Ann*) Oh, I'm so glad you're getting married.

ANN (*kissing her*) Dear Aunt Molly—I didn't want to hurt you.

(MAGGIE *enters down* R)

MISS STANLEY. Oh, Maggie, take my chair in. (*She picks up the table,
with the cards set out on it*)

(MAGGIE *exits down* R *with the chair*)

You mustn't stay out too long, Ann Veronica. When you come in I
want to discuss the question of hymns. I always think *The Voice that
breathed o'er Eden* is a very reliable hymn for a wedding, don't you?

ANN. I'm sure it is. Look, you can put the king on the ace.

MISS STANLEY. So I can. Dear Ann Veronica. I believe it's
coming out after all. (*As she goes* R, *with the table*) Everything comes
out if only you give it time.

(*She exits down* R. ANN *moves down* R *to the seat and sits*)

ANN. But I had no time to wait. I was impatient, and I was
desperate. I saw my life slipping away and wasted, like Aunt
Molly's, and I would never see again the man I loved. I looked out
that night at the slowly circling stars, and watched them counting
the seconds of eternity. I couldn't wait so long.

ANTIGONE

by Sophocles

Translated by Lewis Campbell

The two sons of Oedipus have slain each other in battle and Oedipus's brother-in-law, Creon, ruler of Thebes, issues an edict stating that Eteocles, the younger, shall be decently buried, but Polynices, the elder, left to rot. Antigone, the headstrong younger daughter of Oedipus, tells her gentler sister, Ismene, that she intends to disobey her uncle, Creon.

ANTIGONE. Own sister of my blood, one life with me,
Ismene, have the tidings caught thy ear?
Say, hath not Heaven decreed to execute
On thee and me, while yet we are alive,
All the evil Oedipus bequeathed? All horror
All pain, all outrage, falls on us! And now
The General's proclamation of to-day—
Hast thou not heard?—Art thou so slow to hear
When harm from foes threatens the souls we love?

ISMENE. No word of those we love, Antigone,
Painful or glad, hath reached me, since we two
Were utterly deprived of our two brothers,
Cut off with mutal stroke, both in one day
And since the Argive host this now-past night
Is vanished, I know nought beside to make me
Nearer to happiness or more in woe.

ANTIGONE. I knew it well, and therefore let thee forth
The palace gate that thou alone mightst hear.

ISMENE. Speak on! Thy troubled look bodes some dark news.

ANTIGONE. Why, hath not Creon, in the burial-rite,
Of our two brethren honoured one, and wrought
On one foul wrong? Eteocles, they tell,
With lawful consecration he lays out,
And after covers him in earth, adorned
With amplest honours in the world below.
But Polynices, miserably slain,
They say tis publicly proclaimed that none
Must cover in a grave, nor mourn for him;
But leave him tombless and unwept, a store
Of sweet provision for the carrion fowl
That eye him greedily. Such a righteous law

7

Good Creon hath pronounced for thy behoof—
Ay, and for mine . . . ! I am not left out!—And now
He moves this way to promulgate his will
To such as have not heard, nor lightly holds
The thing he bids, but whoso disobeys,
The citizens shall stone him to the death.
This is the matter, and thou wilt quickly show
If thou art noble, or fallen below thy birth.

ISMENE.   Unhappy one! But what can I herein
Avail to do or undo?

ANTIGONE.   Wilt thou share
The danger and the labour? Make thy choice.

ISMENE.   Of what wild enterprise? What canst thou mean?

ANTIGONE.   Wilt thou join hand with mine to lift the dead?

ISMENE.   To bury him when all have been forbidden?
Is that thy thought?

ANTIGONE.   To bury my own brother
And thine, even though you wilt not do thy part.
I will not be a traitress to my kin.

ISMENE.   Fool-hardy girl! against the word of Creon?

ANTIGONE.   He hath no right to bar me from mine own.

ISMENE.   Ah, sister, think but how our father fell,
Hated of all and lost to fair renown,
Through self-detected crimes,—with his own hand,
Self-wreaking how he dashed out both his eyes:
Then how the mother wife, sad two-fold name!
With twisted halter bruised her life away;
Last, how in one dire moment our two brothers
With internecine conflict at one blow
Wrought out by fratricide their mutual doom.
Now, left alone, O think how beyond all
Most piteously we twain shall be destroyed,
If in defiance of authority
We traverse the commandment of the King!
We needs but bear in mind we are but women,
Never created to contend with men;
Nay more, made victims of resistless power,
To obey behests more harsh than this to-day.
I, then, imploring those beneath to grant
Indulgence, seeing I am enforced in this,
Will yield submission to the powers that rule,
Small wisdom were it to overpass the bound.

ANTIGONE.   I will not urge you! no! nor if now you list
To help me, will your help afford me joy.
Be what you choose to be. This single hand
Shall bury our lost brother. Glorious
For me to take this labour and to die!
Dear to him will my soul be as we rest

In death, when I have dared this holy crime.
My time for pleasing men will soon be over;
Not so my duty toward the Dead! My home
Yonder will have no end. You, if you will,
May pour contempt on laws revered on High.

ISMENE. Not from irreverence. But I have no strength
To strive against the citizens' resolve.

ANTIGONE. Thou, make excuses! I will go my way
To raise a burial-mound to my dear brother.

ISMENE. O hapless maiden, how I fear for thee!

ANTIGONE. Waste not your fears on me! Guide your own fortune.

ISMENE. Ah! yet divulge thine enterprise to none,
But keep the secret close, and so will I.

ANTIGONE. O Heavens! Nay, tell! I hate your silence worse;
I had rather you proclaimed it to the world.

ISMENE. You are ardent in a chilling enterprise.

ANTIGONE. I know that I please those whom I would please.

ISMENE. Yes, if you thrive; but your desire is bootless.

ANTIGONE. Well, when I fail I shall be stopped, I trow!

ISMENE. One should not start upon a hopeless quest,

ANTIGONE. Speak in that vein if you would earn my hate
And aye be hated of our lost one. Peace!
Leave my unwisdom to endure this peril;
Fate cannot rob me of a noble death.

ISMENE. Go, if you must—not to be checked in folly,
But sure unparalleled in faithful love! (*Exeunt*)

ANTIGONE

By Jean Anouilh

Translated by Lewis Galantiere

This depicts the same part of the story as the preceding scene, but is from the French version, written during the German occupation of France.

ISMENE. Aren't you well?

ANTIGONE. Of course I am. Just a little tired. I got up too early. (*She sits on the chair, suddenly tired*)

ISMENE. I couldn't sleep, either.

ANTIGONE. Ismene, you ought not to go without your beauty sleep.

ISMENE. Don't make fun of me.

ANTIGONE. I'm not, Ismene, truly. This particular morning, seeing how beautiful you are makes everything easier for me. Wasn't I a miserable little beast when we were small? I used to fling mud at you, and put worms down your neck. I remember tying you to a tree and cutting off your hair. Your beautiful hair! How easy it must be never to be unreasonable with all that smooth silken hair so beautifully set round your head.

ISMENE (*abruptly*) Why do you insist upon talking about other things?

ANTIGONE (*gently*) I am not talking about other things.

ISMENE. Antigone, I've thought about it a lot.

ANTIGONE. Have you?

ISMENE. I thought about it all night long. Antigone, you're mad.

ANTIGONE. Am I?

ISMENE. We cannot do it.

ANTIGONE. Why not?

ISMENE. Creon will have us put to death.

ANTIGONE. Of course he will. That's what he's here for. He will do what he has to do, and we will do what we have to do. He is bound to put us to death. We are bound to go out and bury our brother. That's the way it is. What do you think we can do to change it?

ISMENE (*releases Antigone's hand; draws back a step*) I don't want to die.

ANTIGONE. I'd prefer not to die, myself.

ISMENE. Listen to me, Antigone. I thought about it all night. I'm older than you are. I always think things over and you don't. You are impulsive. You get a notion in your head and you jump up and do the thing straight off. And if it's silly, well, so much the worse for you. Whereas, *I* think things out.

ANTIGONE. Sometimes it is better not to think too much.

ISMENE. I don't agree with you!

(ANTIGONE *looks at Ismene, then turns and moves*)

Oh, I know it's horrible. And I pity Polynices just as much as you do. But all the same, I sort of see what Uncle Creon means.

ANTIGONE. I don't want to "Sort of see" anything.

ISMENE. Uncle Creon is the king. He has to set an example!

ANTIGONE. But I am not the king; and I don't have to set people examples. Little Antigone gets a notion in her head—the nasty brat, the wilful, wicked girl; and they put her in a corner all day, or they lock her up in the cellar. And she deserves it. She shouldn't have disobeyed!

ISMENE. There you go, frowning, glowering, wanting your own stubborn way in everything. Listen to me. I'm right oftener than you are.

ANTIGONE. I don't want to be right!

ISMENE. At least you can try to understand.

ANTIGONE. Understand! The first word I ever heard out of any of you was that word "understand". Why didn't I "understand" that I must not play with water—cold, black, beautiful flowing water—because I'd spill it on the palace tiles. Or with earth, because earth dirties a little girl's frock. Why didn't I "understand" that nice children don't eat out of every dish at once; or give everything in their pockets to beggars; or run in the wind so fast that they fall down; or ask for a drink when they're perspiring; or want to go swimming when it's either too early or too late, merely because they happen to feel like swimming. Understand! I don't want to understand. There'll be time enough to understand when I'm old. . . . If I ever *am* old. But not now.

ISMENE. He is stronger than we are, Antigone. He is the king. And the whole city is with him. Thousands and thousands of them, swarming through all the streets of Thebes.

ANTIGONE. I am not listening to you.

ISMENE. His mob will come running, howling as it runs. A thousand arms will seize our arms. A thousand breaths will breathe into our faces. Like one single pair of eyes, a thousand eyes will stare at us. We'll be driven in a tumbrel through their hatred, through the smell of them and their cruel, roaring laughter. We'll be dragged to the scaffold for torture, surrounded by guards with their idiot faces all bloated, their animal hands clean-washed for the sacrifice, their beefy eyes squinting as they stare at us. And we'll know that no shrieking and no begging will make them understand that we want to live, for they are like slaves who do exactly as they've been told, without caring about right or wrong. And we shall suffer, we shall feel pain rising in us until it becomes so unbearable that we *know* it must stop. But it won't stop; it will go on rising and rising, like a screaming voice. Oh, I can't, I can't, Antigone! (*A pause*)

ANTIGONE. How well you have thought it all out.

ISMENE. I thought of it all night long. Didn't you?

ANTIGONE. Oh, yes.

ISMENE. I'm an awful coward, Antigone.

ANTIGONE. So am I. But what has that to do with it?

ISMENE. But, Antigone! Don't you want to go on living?

ANTIGONE. Go on living! Who was it that was always the first out of bed because she loved the touch of the cold morning air on her bare skin? Who was always the last to bed because nothing less than infinite weariness could wean her from the lingering night? Who wept when she was little because there were too many grasses in the meadow, too many creatures in the field, for her to know and touch them all?

ISMENE (*claps Antigone's hands, in a sudden rush of tenderness*) Darling little sister!

ANTIGONE (*repulsing her*) No! For heaven's sake! Don't paw me! And don't let us start snivelling! You say you've thought it all out. The howling mob—the torture—the fear of death. . . . They've made up your mind for you. Is that it?

ISMENE. Yes.

ANTIGONE. All right. They're as good excuses as any.

ISMENE. Antigone, be sensible. It's all very well for men to believe in ideas and die for them. But you are a girl!

ANTIGONE. Don't I know I'm a girl? Haven't I spent my life cursing the fact that I was a girl?

ISMENE (*with spirit*) Antigone! You have everything in the world to make you happy. All you have to do is reach out for it. You are going to be married; you are young; you are beautiful . . .

ANTIGONE. I am not beautiful.

ISMENE. Yes, you are! Not the way other girls are. But it's always you that the little boys turn to look back at when they pass us in the street. And when you go by, the little girls stop talking. They stare and stare at you, until we've turned a corner.

ANTIGONE (*a faint smile*) "Little boys—little girls."

ISMENE (*challengingly*) And what about Haemon?

(*Pause*)

ANTIGONE. I shall see Haemon this morning. I'll take care of Haemon. You always said I was mad; and it didn't matter how little I was or what I wanted to do. Go back to bed now, Ismene. The sun is coming up, and, as you see, there is nothing I can do today. Our brother Polynices is as well guarded as if he had won the war and were sitting on his throne. Go along. You are pale with weariness.

ISMENE. What are you going to do?

ANTIGONE. I don't feel like going to bed. However, if you like,

I'll promise not to leave the house till you wake up. Nurse is getting me breakfast. Go and get some sleep. The sun is just up. Look at you: you can't keep your eyes open. Go.

ISMENE. And you will listen to reason, won't you? You'll let me talk to you about this again? Promise?

ANTIGONE. I promise. I'll let you talk. I'll let all of you talk. Go to bed, now.

ISMENE *goes to the arch and exits.*

BACKGROUND

By WARREN CHETHAM-STRODE

Barbara Lomax has parted from her husband, John, and plans to remarry. Nanny Braun, known as Brownie, a middle-aged Austrian woman, realizes the effect the divorce will have on the three children.

SCENE—*The schoolroom of the Lomax's house on the outskirts of London.*
TIME—*1950.*

BARBIE (*sharply*) Why did you leave me? (*She moves to the table down L and takes a handkerchief from her handbag*) I asked you to stay *here.*

BROWNIE (*moving and sitting above the table* RC) I send that hockey stick to Jess. (*She puts the work-basket on the table*) I think that is more important. (*She pauses*) Why you crying, eh?

BARBIE (*drying her eyes*) I don't know. Saying good-bye to someone you've been with all those years—isn't—isn't easy—I suppose. You can't know someone—all that well—without—feeling it.

BROWNIE (*off hand; hunting in the sewing basket*) Then why you do it?

BARBIE (*wearily*) Oh, don't talk like that, Brownie—*please*. (*She pauses and finishes drying her eyes*) John says he'll never marry again.

BROWNIE (*mending a stocking*) Do you blame him? After being married to you I bet he is sick of it.

BARBIE. That wasn't the reason he gave me. That's what really upset me.

BROWNIE (*looking at her*) You better go wash your face. Otherwise you lose the other one too.

BARBIE. Bill doesn't mind what I look like. He loves me.

BROWNIE. He won't love you if you are crying over another man.

BARBIE. I'm *not* crying over another man. John's my husband.

(*There is a pause.* BROWNIE *goes on sewing*)

Things always happen at the same time, don't they? I'm miserable about seeing the children off to school—then I have to say good-bye to John.

BROWNIE (*cynically*) You have a lot of self-pity for yourself—eh? You are very hard treated—no? *Poor* Barbie.

BARBIE. You're awfully unkind sometimes, aren't you?

BROWNIE. Sometimes—when I am very angry inside.

BARBIE. What are you angry about?

BROWNIE (*calmly*) Mustn't no-one be angry but you? (*She pauses*) Have you had letter from Adrian—how is his cold?

BARBIE. I haven't heard. They write on Sundays. (*She moves to the*

14

table down L, *picks up her handbag and puts her handkerchief in it*) That reminds me. (*She digs into her bag*) Has Adrian still got that childish habit of playing with matches?

BROWNIE. I stop him doing that—why?

BARBIE. When I was emptying the waste-paper basket in his room this morning—I found that. (*She produces the charred corner of a five-pound note*)

BROWNIE. What is that?

BARBIE (*moving to* L *of the table* RC) The corner of a five-pound note. It's been burnt.

BROWNIE. How has he got a five-pound note?

BARBIE. His grannie sent him one last Christmas. But I *thought* he put it in the Post Office. (*She replaces the charred note in her handbag*)

BROWNIE. I suppose he have an accident.

BARBIE (*moving to the table down* L) Rather an expensive one. (*She puts her handbag on the table*)

BROWNIE. And he is too proud to speak about it? Oh, well—it is his own fault to be so silly.

BARBIE (*after a pause*) Why are you angry, Brownie? You didn't tell me.

BROWNIE (*after a pause*) When I am angry—I do not speak. When *you* are angry—you talk too much, That is the difference.

BARBIE (*perching herself on the* R *arm of the armchair*) You might tell me what it's about.

(*There is a pause.* BROWNIE *finds another hole in the stocking*)

BROWNIE. What you talk with Mr John about—just now?

BARBIE (*casually*) About ourselves, chiefly. He's got a very important case on tomorrow. It means a lot to him.

BROWNIE. And *what* did you talk about *yourself*.

BARBIE. Nothing much. About marriage in general.

BROWNIE (*casually*) You talk a lot about yourselves—but you don't talk about the children? Eh?

BARBIE. Not then, Brownie, no, but we're always worrying about them and watching them.

BROWNIE. You are watching them—but you not notice things about Jess this last month?

BARBIE (*after a pause*) What sort of things? (*She pauses*) She's been rather stupid once or twice. That business over the horse and the bicycle—d'you mean that?

BROWNIE. That girl is bad—ever since she was tiny she has bad streak in her.

BARBIE (*surprised and annoyed*) What nonsense!

BROWNIE. All right. You see. All her life I try to bring her up good—because *I know* there is bad things in her. But now she has no home—you will see she will get badder and badder—and when she grow up you have a lot of troubles with her.

BARBIE. But she *has* got a home.

BROWNIE. She will have two *houses*—but she has no longer got a home. There is a big difference.

BARBIE. It's absurd to talk like that, Brownie—quite absurd—she'll . . .

BROWNIE. Then why does Linda cry herself to sleep in my arms? Two nights last week she come into my bed and cry and cry and cry. "We have no home, Brownie—no home any more," she say.

(*There is a pause as* BARBIE *rises and moves* L *of the table* RC)

BARBIE (*sharply*) Why didn't you tell me this before?

BROWNIE. Because she speak private to me.

BARBIE. That's ridiculous. I should have been told.

BROWNIE. What could you do—if I tell you? Would you not go away with Mr Bill?

BARBIE (*after a pause*) Of course I'm going away with Bill—but (*agitated and worried*) I could have explained things to Linda. I could have . . .

BROWNIE. You have explained once already. What is the good of explaining more? You have decided to do this thing—you must take what happens.

BARBIE (*defiantly*) What will happen?

BROWNIE. How do I know?

BARBIE. Then why are you saying these things?

BROWNIE. Because I see what happens to other children.

BARBIE. I've known several women with children, who've had divorces. They've managed all right.

BROWNIE (*after a pause*) And the children? Have they been all right?

BARBIE (*after a pause; defensively*). Perfectly.

BROWNIE (*with a shrug*) It may be good with some children, I don't know. But with *these* children—it will never be good. That I am sure.

BARBIE (*turning and moving to the fireplace*) I don't think you've any right to say that, Brownie.

BROWNIE (*suddenly angry*) I don't care what right I have—I say it. (*She pauses*) I have just come back from Germany.

BARBIE (*sitting in the armchair*) What's that got to do with it?

(*There is a pause*)

BROWNIE. I stay here with my sister, as you know. (*She pauses*) She has four children—she used to have five. The eldest one, Fritz, the Russians they took him away. (*She breaks the darning wool with a twirl of her fingers*) So for them he is dead.

BARBIE (*sympathetically*) Your sister's had a terrible time, I know. But I don't quite see . . . (*She breaks off*)

(BROWNIE *picks up another stocking. Her voice is quite calm and unemotional*)

BROWNIE. My sister, and her husband, they live in a cellar. Her man, he works in the Deutsch Bank. He does not earn much money, and prices of food and things are high. So, you would think with all these troubles that the children are getting bad—for nothing is left of all the safe things my sister used to know—nothing at all. (*She pauses*) But no. (*She pauses*) The girls are good girls—the boy is a fine boy—he is going to work this summer. How is that happen, eh? Because of *one* thing. They have a mudder and fader—who have made for them a home in a cellar.

BARBIE. Why are you telling me this?

BROWNIE (*her voice rising*) Because you ask me why I am angry. (*Slowly*) I have never been so angry in all my life.

BARBIE (*after a pause*) But, Brownie . . .

BROWNIE (*putting down her sewing; her voice low and intense*) Who are you to do this thing? *Your* life does not matter any more—you have made it for good or bad—but it is made. The children's is *not* made.

BARBIE (*rising and moving* C) But, Brownie, because I have children you can't tell me my own life's finished. That's sheer nonsense and you know it. If the children are unhappy now it is because they are too young to understand the situation. But I believe, in the long run, they'll be far happier when they realize that their parents decided to separate instead of scrapping every hour of the day and making their lives hell, too.

BROWNIE (*sharply*) Listen to me, Barbie. Everywhere in the world today is troubles—nothing but troubles. What can you give your children today, that will make them happy. Money? No. Security? No—there is no security. What is there you can give them? *One* thing—and *that* you have taken away—because you are sorry for yourselves, and think of no-one else but John and Barbie.

BARBIE. What do you *mean?*

BROWNIE. I mean a word I cannot think of now—but it will come. It means love and a good home—it means safety and happiness—it means all dose things children must have, if they are to grow into decent human beings—(*her voice rises*) and that's what you have taken away from Jess and Adrian and Linda—that's—(*she pauses*) I know the word now, I remember. (*She pauses*) It is called—background. That is the most precious thing in life a child can have—and you have destroyed it for them, Barbie. (*She pauses. Slowly and quietly*) That is what you have done.

BARBIE (*very upset*) You only think that because you *want* to think it, and because you won't *try* and see my point of view. You're saying all this to stop me, but nothing will stop me—because I can't stand this atmosphere any longer. You don't know what it is to be always on the defence—always being put in the wrong whether I am or not —and I can't go on any longer, Brownie—I can't go on any longer, I'm tired of *battling*. (*She pauses. She is more upset*) You can think what you like and say what you like—but I've made up my mind. John doesn't want me any more, and whatever happens, I'm going to Bill. So please—*please* don't start again.

(*The telephone begins to ring*)

BROWNIE (*after a moment; making a slight move*) Shall I answer?
BARBIE (*with an effort*) No. (*She crosses to the door down* R, *walking like a tired woman*) I'll go.

(*She exits down* R, *leaves the door open, and lifts the telephone receiver*)

(*Off. Into the telephone*) Hullo? . . . Yes—this is Mrs Lomax speaking.

(*She re-enters down* R, *trailing the flex and carrying the instrument*)

It's a trunk call. (*She sits* R *of the table* RC)
BROWNIE (*rising and putting the darning in the basket*) Shall I make some tea for you and Mr Bill?
BARBIE (*her mind elsewhere*) What did you say?
BROWNIE (*louder*) I say shall I make a cup of tea for you and Mr Bill, when he comes for you?
BARBIE (*not looking at Brownie*) Yes—will you please. Thank you. (*Into the telephone*) Hullo? . . . Yes, speaking . . . Oh, good afternoon . . . How's Adrian? . . . But I don't understand . . . He—he *hasn't* . . . But he left three days ago . . . What? . . . (*She is obviously frightened*) But I can't understand it . . . No, I've had no letter . . . You've done that, you say? . . . Oh, you *will* do it? . . . Yes, I think that's right . . . Yes, yes, I'll ring my husband at once, of course . . . And you'll ring me if . . . Thank you very much . . . Good-bye. (*She slowly replaces the receiver and stares out front*) Adrian hasn't arrived at school—and he left three days ago.

BROWNIE *stares at Barbie as—*

the CURTAIN *falls*

BERNADETTE

By Noel Woolf and Sheila Buckley

Based on an original play by Martin Adeson

Bernadette Soubirous, the simple, delicate peasant girl, has entered the Convent of the Sisters of Charity, after her visions of "the beautiful lady" in the Grotto at Lourdes. Her life as a nun is under the guidance of the intelligent and severe Mother Marie-Thérèse who is sceptical of the authenticity of her apparitions.

Scene—*The Infirmarian's office at the Convent at Nevers.*
Time—*1866.*

MARIE-THÉRÈSE. Sister Marie-Bernard, permission has been granted for you to meet a Franciscan father who is visiting Nevers. He is here now, and you will be sent for when he is ready to receive you. Until then you may spend the time recapturing the memories of your life in Lourdes.

BERNADETTE. I don't need any time to remember them.

MARIE-THÉRÈSE (*moving up* R) He will wish to question you and any discrepancies in your story will look bad.

BERNADETTE. Whatever he asks me I will tell him—with the Reverend Mother's permission, of course.

MARIE-THÉRÈSE (*turning to her*) Of course. For this occasion you have permission. But at no other time. Is that clear?

BERNADETTE (*moving a few steps to* LC) I have never spoken of that life, except under obedience, since I came here.

MARIE-THÉRÈSE. Are you quite sure?

BERNADETTE. I know how to hold my tongue.

MARIE-THÉRÈSE (*coming down below the chair* R *of the table*) And I know what chatterboxes you peasant girls can be.

BERNADETTE. I have never lied to you. Because we were poor and mother took in washing, it doesn't mean we were brought up to lie and cheat. Mother has always been as strict as you are . . .

MARIE-THÉRÈSE. I seem to remember your father was in prison once. (*She sits* R *of the table*)

BERNADETTE. There is no shame in that. The poor are often in prison. I'm proud of my father; and my mother never let us go dirty or untidy if she could help it.

MARIE-THÉRÈSE. Pride, Sister, pride . . .

BERNADETTE. God tells us to honour our father and mother; there cannot be sin in that.

MARIE-THÉRÈSE. And did your Lady tell you to defy authority?

BERNADETTE. Must you remind me! I shall never see Lourdes again nor my Lady, until I die. (*She sits* L *of the table*) It's so lonely. I know I must speak of these things under obedience, but not now. Please not now. Please, please let me keep them to myself.

MARIE-THÉRÈSE. The privilege you were granted was a very great one. It cannot have been meant for you alone. Your Lady would not want you to keep those wonderful secrets to yourself if they could help others. She would not wish you to be selfish.

BERNADETTE (*wearily; this is not the first time the conversation has taken this trend*) She told me what I was to keep to myself and what I was to tell others. I have told you everything I am allowed.

MARIE-THÉRÈSE. Have you? Are you quite sure? Think how dreadful it would be if your memory were to play you false.

BERNADETTE. My Lady would not allow me to forget anything.

MARIE-THÉRÈSE (*rising*) Do you think the Mother of God has nothing better to do than jog your memory for you?

BERNADETTE (*obstinately*) I know my Lady would never break a promise. And I shall never tell the secrets she gave to me.

MARIE-THÉRÈSE. No, I don't think you will. (*She looks at Bernadette long and searchingly*) Are they to die with you?

(BERNADETTE *is silent*)

(*As she speaks she moves round above the table to* L *of Bernadette*) If you were given some special knowledge I should have thought it would have been your duty to keep it in this world. (*She is tempting her to speak*)

(BERNADETTE *is still silent*)

(*Becoming exasperated*) When I think of the things you are supposed to have been told, and the little you have done, I tremble for the fate of your soul.

BERNADETTE. I don't know why my Lady chose me, but she did. And she knows I have done all she asked of me. Now I have only to suffer, and pray for sinners.

MARIE-THÉRÈSE. Take care, child, take care.

BERNADETTE. With your help, Mother, I will try to be worthy of my Lady.

(*For a moment* MARIE-THÉRÈSE *looks deeply into Bernadette's face*)

MARIE-THÉRÈSE (*almost to herself*) Those eyes . . . Those eyes . . . O God . . . Pride, my daughter; pride; let there be no place for it in your soul. Cast it out.

BERNADETTE (*in a whisper*) Yes, Mother.

MARIE-THÉRÈSE. You must be proud, you must. You who have . . . (*She crosses above the table to* RC; *her voice hardens*) You have touched rosaries and given the trimmings of your hair for keepsakes . . . (*Turning*) If you are not proud why did you do these things? Why?

BERNADETTE. It made people happy.

MARIE-THÉRÈSE. And do you still do it?

BERNADETTE. No. It meant nothing.

MARIE-THÉRÈSE (*moving in to* R *of the table*) Are you sure? Are you quite sure?

BERNADETTE. I have been forbidden.

MARIE-THÉRÈSE (*crossing below the table to* L) You might do it for a novice, if it means nothing.

BERNADETTE. They never speak of Lourdes.

MARIE-THÉRÈSE (*turning*) How do you know? Do you know more about them than I do? (*Looking at the door* L) There's one of them here now might ask you to bless her new rosary . . .

BERNADETTE. I wouldn't do anything so blasphemous. I have never blessed a rosary.

MARIE-THÉRÈSE (*closing in to her*)˙ When you touched them, what were you doing then?

BERNADETTE. I have told you, Mother, I only did it to give a friend a present—a remembrance; I hoped they would pray for me.

MARIE-THÉRÈSE (*moving behind her*) And what sort of present was your touch? And what about your hair?

BERNADETTE. Please! (*She rises*) You make my head go round and round as if you were trying to trap me.

MARIE-THÉRÈSE (*turning above the table*) If you can think that of your Novice Mistress it only goes to show how far you have to travel. (*She sits above the table*)

BERNADETTE. Yes, Mother.

(*For the moment it seems there is nothing more to be said*)

MARIE-THÉRÈSE (*holding out the rosary*) Do you recognize this?

BERNADETTE (*turning and breaking away a little*) No.

MARIE-THÉRÈSE. You have never seen it before? You are sure? Look closely at it.

(BERNADETTE *steps forward to look at it*)

It means nothing to you?

BERNADETTE. Why should it?

MARIE-THÉRÈSE. Because it belonged to Marie-Raphael.

BERNADETTE. The one that Reverend Mother took away from her?

MARIE-THÉRÈSE. So you knew that?

BERNADETTE. She told me. It made her cry.

MARIE-THÉRÈSE. And why should it make her cry? What is so special about this rosary?

BERNADETTE. I don't know. Did her mother give it to her? Or perhaps she had it for her First Communion.

MARIE-THÉRÈSE. You know that was not the reason. You know very well why she was so distressed at parting with it. Because you had touched it.

BERNADETTE. Oh, no! (*She backs away up* L) But I touched so many. I didn't know. Please may she have it back. Please! If I had known it could ever make her unhappy . . .

MARIE-THÉRÈSE. You see now the harm you have done? No, she will not have it back. (*She puts it away inside her habit*) Such relics of hysteria and exhibitionism have no place in a convent.

BERNADETTE (*coming down* LC) When first I came here I felt happiness and peace all around, warming me like sunshine. I thought . . . I thought . . . (*But she cannot voice her thought*) How hard life can be, even in the sun.

MARIE-THÉRÈSE. All life is hard. From birth to death for everyone it's a battlefield. (*She rises and comes down to* R *of Bernadette*) But some of us have been chosen by God to fight for the souls of others as well as for our own. I have fought for you, Sister Marie-Bernard, and I will continue to fight, that in the end you may be won for God.

BERNADETTE (*turning to her*) Fight for me, Mother, yes, if you must, but pray for me, too. I have great need of prayers—your prayers.

MARIE-THÉRÈSE. Whatever the Lady of your visions—if they were visions—promised, Heaven is not in your pocket.

BERNADETTE (*turning away*) She never promised me Heaven. And I know I shall not go there unless I pray and suffer well in this life. (*Turning to her*) But they were real, the visions, I know they were. I know it. I know it . . .

MARIE-THÉRÈSE (*facing her*) If you are so sure, why must you keep telling yourself so?

BERNADETTE. I am sure. I am. It is you I am telling. You are the one who is not sure.

THE CHALK GARDEN

By Enid Bagnold

Laurel, sixteen, highly strung and over-imaginative, lives in her grand-mother's eccentric household; one after the other her governess-companions leave her, but when the astute, enigmatic Miss Madrigal arrives, Laurel meets her match.

SCENE—*A room in the house of Laurel's grandmother.*
PERIOD—*Modern.*

LAUREL (*moving to R of the table*) So you've been to a trial?
MADRIGAL (*crossing to the couch*) I did not say I hadn't.
LAUREL (*moving to L of Madrigal*) Why did you not say—when you know what store we both lay by it?
MADRIGAL (*picking up the paintings from the floor*) It may be I think you lay too much store by it. (*She puts the paintings on the table below the couch*)
LAUREL (*relaxing her tone and asking as though an ordinary light question*) How does one get in?
MADRIGAL. It's surprisingly easy. (*She sits on the couch and picks up the paintbox*)
LAUREL. Was it a trial for murder?
MADRIGAL (*closing the box*) It would have to be to satisfy you.
LAUREL. *Was* it a trial for murder?
MADRIGAL (*picking up Laurel's painting block*) Have you finished that flower?
LAUREL (*yawning*) As much as I can. I get tired of it. (*Wandering to the window*) In my house—at home—there were so many things to do.
MADRIGAL. What was it like?
LAUREL. My home? (*She moves the small table by the couch and sets it R of the armchair*)
MADRIGAL. Yes.
LAUREL (*as though caught unaware*) There was a stream. And a Chinese bridge. And yew trees cut like horses. And a bell on the weathervane, and a little wood called mine . . .
MADRIGAL. Who called it that?
LAUREL (*unwillingly moved*) She did. My mother. And when it was raining we made an army of her cream pots and a battlefield of her dressing-table—I used to thread her rings on safety pins . . .
MADRIGAL. Tomorrow I will light that candle in the green glass candlestick and you can try to paint that.

23

LAUREL. What—paint the flame? (*She collects the loose paintings and the jar of water and puts them on the table up* C)

MADRIGAL. Yes.

LAUREL (*putting the vase and rose on the desk*) I'm tired of fire, too, Boss.

MADRIGAL (*putting the painting book on the downstage end of the couch*) Why do you sign your name a thousand times?

LAUREL. I am looking for which is me.

MADRIGAL. Shall we read?

LAUREL (*sitting on the desk chair*) Oh, I don't want to read.

MADRIGAL. Let's have a game.

LAUREL. All right. (*With meaning*) A *guessing* game.

MADRIGAL. Very well. Do you know one?

LAUREL (*rising and moving above the armchair*) Maitland and I play one called "The Sky's the Limit".

MADRIGAL. How do you begin?

(LAUREL *takes the cushion from the armchair, puts it on the floor beside the couch and sits on it*)

LAUREL. We ask three questions each but if you don't answer one, I get a fourth.

MADRIGAL. What do we guess about?

LAUREL. Let's guess about each other. We are both mysterious . . .

MADRIGAL (*sententious*) The human heart is mysterious.

LAUREL. We don't know the first thing about each other, so there are so many things to ask.

MADRIGAL. But we mustn't go too fast. Or there will be nothing left to discover. Has it got to be the truth?

LAUREL. One can lie. But I get better and better at spotting lies. It's so dull playing with Maitland. He's so innocent.

(MADRIGAL *folds her hands and waits*)

Now! First question. Are you a—*maiden* lady?

MADRIGAL (*after a moment's reflection*) I can't answer that.

LAUREL. Why?

MADRIGAL. Because you throw the emphasis so oddly.

LAUREL. Right! You don't answer. So now I have an extra question. (*She pauses*) Are you living under an assumed name?

MADRIGAL. No.

LAUREL. Careful! I'm getting my lie-detector working. Do you take things here at their face value?

MADRIGAL. No.

LAUREL. Splendid! You're getting the idea.

MADRIGAL (*warningly*) This is to be your fourth question.

LAUREL (*rising, moving* C *and turning*) Yes. Yes, indeed. I must think—I must be careful. (*She shoots her question hard at Madrigal*) What is the full name of your married sister?

(MADRIGAL *covers the paintbox with her hand and stares for a brief second at Laurel*)

MADRIGAL. Clarissa Dalrymple Westerham.

LAUREL. Is Dalrymple Westerham a double name?

MADRIGAL (*with ironical satisfaction*) You've *had* your questions.

LAUREL (*gaily accepting defeat*) Yes, I have. Now yours. You've only three unless I pass one. (*She resumes her seat on the cushion*)

MADRIGAL (*after a pause*) Was your famous affair in Hyde Park on the night of your mother's marriage?

LAUREL (*wary*) About that time.

MADRIGAL. What was the charge by the police?

LAUREL (*wary*) The police didn't come into it.

MADRIGAL (*airily*) Did someone follow you? And try to kiss you?

LAUREL (*off her guard*) Kiss me! It was a case of Criminal Assault.

MADRIGAL (*following that up*) How do you know—if there wasn't a charge by the Police?

LAUREL (*after a brief pause; triumphant*) That's one too many questions. (*She rises*) Now for the deduction. (*She picks up the cushion, replaces it on the armchair and sits*)

MADRIGAL. You didn't tell me there was a deduction.

LAUREL. I forgot. It's the whole point. Mine's ready.

MADRIGAL. What do you deduce?

LAUREL (*taking a breath; then fast, as though she might be stopped*) That you've changed so much you must have been something quite different. When you came here you were like a rusty hinge that wanted oiling. You spoke to yourself out loud without knowing it. You had been *alone*. You may have been a missionary in Central Africa. You may have escaped from a private asylum. But as a maiden lady you are an impostor. (*She changes her tone slightly; slower and more penetrating*) About your assumed name I am not so sure. *But you have no married sister.*

MADRIGAL (*lightly*) You take my breath away.

LAUREL (*leaning back in her chair; as lightly*) Good at it, aren't I?

MADRIGAL (*gaily*) Yes, for a mind under a cloud.

LAUREL. Now for *your* deduction.

MADRIGAL (*rising*) Mine must keep. (*She moves to the door down* R, *taking the paintbox with her*)

LAUREL (*rising*) But it's the game! Where are you going?

MADRIGAL (*pleasantly*) To my room. To be sure I have left no clues unlocked. (*She opens the door*)

LAUREL. To your past life?

MADRIGAL. Yes. You have given me so much warning.

DARK BETROTHAL

By T. B. Morris

Elizabeth of York, a restrained, gentle girl, is waiting with her younger, impulsive sister, Cecilia, for news of the Battle of Bosworth.

SCENE—*A room in the Manor House of Sheriff Hutton, Yorkshire.*
TIME—*Late August 1485.*

ELIZABETH. It is getting late.

CECILIA (*at the window*) And no messenger yet.

ELIZABETH (*wearily*) Nothing more than the rumour of a great battle to the south.

CECILIA (*turning to face Elizabeth*) Oh, we know that! Rumours that kill one another—now York has triumphed, now Lancaster! . . . Are we to have another night of horror? . . . God! when shall we know *more?*

ELIZABETH (*calmly*) *Trust* God, sister, and have patience.

CECILIA. We don't even know whether the battle is over. All those men—like wolves at one another's throats, and you counsel—patience! . . .

ELIZABETH. I also counselled trust in God.

(CECILIA *moves abruptly down stage and takes up the sword from the bench*)

CECILIA (*bitterly*) When He taught men to make—this. (*She pulls the sword a little from its scabbard. It is too long for her to draw fully, and its weight must be apparent in her hands, providing sharp contrast*) Look at it! There are bloodstains on it yet.

(CECILIA *goes to the* R *side of the dais, holding the sword across her outstretched hands.* ELIZABETH *remains calm and sad*)

CECILIA. Look! And think of it—thousands of these beating out the lives of men . . . Ay, and worse! That dreadful gunpowder—tearing men in pieces—like a beast, but more deadly—invisible . ..

ELIZABETH (*with sudden authority*) Don't! . . . We have our thoughts. Let them suffice for horror.

CECILIA. Oh, how can you be so calm, Elizabeth? One would think you didn't care—(*hysterically*) didn't care that men are butchering one another in this dreadful quarrel for the throne of England—that, whether York or Lancaster is victorious, *we*—are in peril . . .

ELIZABETH. Be quiet, Cecilia! . . .

CECILIA. But pray God our Uncle Richard is killed . . .

ELIZABETH. I tell you to be quiet . . .

CECILIA (*interrupting*) Oh! the thought of him fills me with terror . . . Every night I lie awake in the dark, listening—listening for the soft tread of murderers, coming to stifle me as they stifled our brothers in the Tower—by *his* order . . .

ELIZABETH (*sharply*) Cecilia! . . .

CECILIA. We are in his way, Elizabeth. If he wins this battle he will send to this place—to this *prison*—and . . .

(CECILIA, *by this time sobbing again with fear, sinks to her knees, still clasping the sword.* ELIZABETH, *who is making a great effort for control, rises and moves quietly to the window, looking out, forcing herself to speak calmly*)

ELIZABETH. So peaceful it looks, towards the south . . . But the battle is—or was—far away from here. . . .

CECILIA (*passionately*) Is—or was. . . . Our fate may be already set . . . Which will you have—a tyrant who professes friendship and intends murder; or a sworn enemy who hates bitterly all our house?

(ELIZABETH *becomes suddenly tense, her hands clenched*)

Oh, a pretty choice! But you do not think of that! You have no feeling—no imagination! You have . . .

(ELIZABETH *turns on Cecilia, herself suddenly losing control*)

ELIZABETH. Stop, you little fool! *I* do not think of it? I do not care—I? . . . What are *your* little fears to place against mine? . . .

CECILIA. *Little* fears! But Uncle Richard will murder us! Why else did he send us here? . . .

ELIZABETH. I will tell you why he sent us here . . . (*Slowly and bitterly*) Because he would have married *me*. . . .

CECILIA (*reacting*) You? . . .

ELIZABETH. Me—*his niece.* Because my title to the throne of England is greater than his . . . Why do you suppose he took us to Court—made much of me—gave me dresses just like those of his poor unfortunate Queen who died of grief? . . . Have you ever thought of that?

CECILIA. Oh-h! . . .

ELIZABETH. You have no more than *death* to fear. But I—I have a great dread of *life.*

(*Pause.* CECILIA *is horrified*)

CECILIA. Then you should the more pray for Uncle Richard's death . . .

ELIZABETH. Which will deliver me into the arms of Henry Tudor, whose purpose is the same—to marry me and strengthen his title to the throne. . . . *I* do not care, you say, whether York or Lancaster wins this battle! I do not care—when *my* fate is—to be married to the victor! . . .

CECILIA. But not—your uncle! That would be sinful. . . . And his hands drip murder—his own brother—our brothers—his wife . . .

ELIZABETH (*bitterly*) Oh! Dispensations from Rome cover all the sins of kings.

CECILIA. But—uncle and niece. . . . Our mother, surely, would never allow such a marriage . . . (*Pause*)

ELIZABETH (*pointedly*) Have you ever known our mother refuse to do anything—*anything*—that would give her power, position, wealth? Has she not always intrigued to be on the winning side? Did she not force us to go with her to Court—to the Court of a king who had murdered her own sons?

CECILIA (*horrified*) Elizabeth! . . .

ELIZABETH (*quietly*) I have refused to speak of it. I have shuddered even to let the thought into my mind—but your fearful tongue has unlocked the way for it. . . . Our mother would never scruple to use my heart as a stepping-stone to power—or my honour—or yours . . .

CECILIA (*beginning to cry again*) Oh-h-h! . . .

ELIZABETH. That is why I say, trust in God. Without Him we are utterly alone. And stop crying, girl. Remember who you are.

CECILIA (*drying her eyes*) I—I've tried to remember that, Elizabeth. But I—I'm not brave like you are, and . . .

ELIZABETH (*firmly*) Be quiet! I am not brave . . .

THE FAN

By Carlo Goldoni

Translated by Eleanor and Herbert Farjeon

Candida has seen her love, Evaristo, give to Giannina, a peasant girl, a fan which she had hoped would come to her to replace a broken one. Mistakenly she takes this as a sign that Evaristo is deceiving her and is determined to find out from the gossipy shopkeeper, Susanna.

SCENE—*Casa Nuove, a village near Milan.*
TIME—*18th century.*

Enter CANDIDA *from the villa.*

CANDIDA. I shall not rest till I get to the bottom of this. I saw Evaristo come out of the shop and then go to Giannina; and that he gave her something I am convinced. I will see whether Susanna cannot enlighten me. My aunt was right: never trust anyone you don't know through and through. Alas, if he should prove faithless! My first—my only love! (*Approaching Susanna as she speaks*)

SUSANNA (*rising*) Oh, Signora Candida! your humble servant.

CANDIDA. Good day, Signora Susanna. What pretty work have you in hand there?

SUSANNA. Oh, I am only running up a cap to pass the time.

CANDIDA. For sale?

SUSANNA. For sale, but heaven knows when.

CANDIDA. I may be wanting a nightcap myself.

SUSANNA. I have some already finished. Would you like to see them?

CANDIDA. No, no, not now, some other time.

SUSANNA. Would you care to take a seat? (*Offering her a chair*)

CANDIDA. But you . . . ?

SUSANNA. Oh, I'll fetch another chair. (*She goes into the shop and brings out a cane chair*) Take this one, it's more comfortable.

CANDIDA. Pray be seated also, and continue working. (*She seats herself*)

SUSANNA. I'm glad you don't feel yourself above my company. (*She sits*) That shows your good breeding. Well-bred people aren't above anything, whereas these yokels are as proud as Lucifer; and as for that Giannina . . .

CANDIDA. Talking of Giannina, did you observe her when she was speaking with Signor Evaristo?

SUSANNA. Observe her? I should think I did!

CANDIDA. They had quite a long chat together.

SUSANNA. And do you know what happened afterwards? Do you know about the rumpus?

CANDIDA. I heard a lot of noise and quarrelling. I was told that Coronato and Crespino tried to fight.

SUSANNA. Just so, and all on account of that precious beauty.

CANDIDA. But why?

SUSANNA. Jealous of each other, and jealous of Signor Evaristo.

CANDIDA. Then, do you believe that Signor Evaristo is attracted to Giannina?

SUSANNA. I know nothing at all, it's not my way to meddle in other people's affairs, I never think ill of anybody; but if the innkeeper and the cobbler *are* jealous of him—no doubt they have their reasons!

CANDIDA (*aside*) Alas, I have my reasons, too!

SUSANNA. Pardon me! I trust that I have not been indiscreet?

CANDIDA. In what way?

SUSANNA. I trust that you yourself have no affection for Signor Evaristo.

CANDIDA. What! I? He is nothing to me. I am acquainted with him, because he comes occasionally to the house; but he is my aunt's friend.

SUSANNA. Then I will tell you the truth. (*Aside*) I don't think she can take it amiss. (*To Candida*) I half thought that there was some sort of understanding between you and Signor Evaristo. . . . Oh, quite as it should be, of course; but after his visit to me this morning, I was completely undeceived.

CANDIDA. He visited you this morning?

SUSANNA. As I'm telling you, Signora. . . . He came to buy a fan.

CANDIDA (*anxiously*) He bought a fan?

SUSANNA. Just so; and as I had seen how yours had been broken, partly on Signor Evaristo's account, I said to myself at once: He is buying this for Signora Candida.

CANDIDA. Then he did buy it for me?

SUSANNA. Oh, no, Signora. I made so bold as to ask him if he was buying it for you. And as I live, he answered, as though he was very much put out: Not at all, he said; what have I to do with Signora Candida? It's for somebody else.

CANDIDA. And what did he do with the fan?

SUSANNA. What did he do with it! He presented it to Giannina.

CANDIDA (*agitated*) All is lost! I am undone!

SUSANNA (*observing her agitation*) Signora Candida!

CANDIDA. False! Faithless! And for whom? A mere peasant-girl!

SUSANNA (*with concern*) Signora Candida!

CANDIDA. The insult is past all bearing!

SUSANNA (*aside*) Mercy! now I've done it! Signora, compose yourself. There may be some mistake.

CANDIDA. You believe he gave the fan to Giannina?

SUSANNA. Oh, as to that, I saw it with my own eyes.

CANDIDA. And yet you say there may be some mistake?

SUSANNA. I don't know. . . . I shouldn't like to be the cause of . . .

(GELTRUDE *appears at the door of the villa*)

SUSANNA (*to Candida*) Oh, here is your aunt.

CANDIDA (*to Susanna*) For heaven's sake, tell her nothing!

SUSANNA. No fear of that. (*Aside*) And she said he was nothing to her! It's her own fault; why couldn't she tell me the truth?

FIVE FINGER EXERCISE

By Peter Shaffer

Walter, the young German tutor, unsettles the Harrington household, and Louise, feeling that her own family do not appreciate her artistic taste, is attracted to him. Pamela, her lively, intelligent fourteen-year-old daughter, is very perceptive.

Scene—*The Harrington's week-end cottage, Suffolk.*
Period—*Modern.*

Louise. Now—sit down. (*She puts Pamela's crop, cap and tin on the table and her coat on the chair R of the table*)

(Pamela *sits* L *of the table*)

(*She examines Pamela's head*) Let me see. Does it hurt?
Pamela. No, it doesn't.
Louise. You say that as if you wanted it to. What on earth were you doing?
Pamela (*exasperated*) Nothing. I just tripped on that stupid coat. And that idiot Walter has to come in and pick me up as if I was a chandelier or something. Holding me that way.
Louise (*carefully*) What way, darling?
Pamela. Well, trying to carry me, as if I was a baby.
Louise (*crossing above Pamela to* L *of her*) But he was only trying to help you—wasn't he?
Pamela (*angrily*) I think he's just plain soppy.
Louise. Because he was worried about you?
Pamela. Oh, Mother, for heaven's sake! You don't understand anything. It's just so *undignified*, can't you see? It shows no *respect* for you. I mean, if you're two years old it's all right to pick you off floors that way, and even then it's an invasion of your privacy. If children of two could speak, you know what they'd say: "Why can't you keep your filthy hands to yourself?"

(Louise *crosses behind Pamela, picks up the cap, crop and tin from the table and Pamela's jersey from the chair* R)

Louise. I think you'd better be off on your ride before you get into any more trouble.

(Pamela *rises and moves towards the schoolroom stairs*)

(*She picks up the coat and hands it to Pamela*) Here—take this.

PAMELA (*going down the stairs to the landing*) Oh, it's one of those mornings.

(*The lights in the schoolroom fade to a half*)

I bet you anything the horse breaks its leg.

(LOUISE *follows Pamela on to the landing. As they reach the landing the music from Walter's room recommences*)

D'you think Walter heard what I was saying just now?

LOUISE (R *of Pamela*) Well, you weren't exactly whispering, were you? Now, come along.

(LOUISE *and* PAMELA *go down the stairs and into the living-room. While they are on their way and the stage is empty, the gramophone record sticks. The passage is repeated four times, then the needle is moved on*)

PAMELA (*moving down* LC) I think I'm the most impossible person I know.

(LOUISE *leaves the hall door open and crosses to* R *of Pamela*)

But then I suppose wonderful people always make you feel like that. Sort of ashamed all the time.

LOUISE. He makes you feel ashamed?

PAMELA (*taking her cap from Louise*) Not exactly ashamed, but, well, like in those advertisements for washing powder. I always feel like the grubby shirt next to the dazzling white one. (*She puts on her cap*) He's so fresh. Fresh and beautiful. (*Brightly*) Don't you think he's beautiful?

LOUISE (*handing Pamela the crop and sandwich tin; confused*) I hadn't thought.

PAMELA. It's just what he is. (*She picks up the newspaper from the floor and puts it on the bench*) He should wear a frock-coat and have consumption.

LOUISE. What nonsense.

PAMELA. Why? There *are* people like that.

LOUISE (*with sudden irritation*) Well, Walter certainly isn't one of them. He's obviously quite a happy, normal·young man. There's simply no reason for you to weave any romantic ideas about him being tragic or different in any way.

PAMELA (*moving down* L; *grandly*) I'm afraid it's obvious you don't know him very well.

(LOUISE *is unamused. Instead, she is making an effort at self-control*)

LOUISE. If you're going, you'd better go. (*She holds out the jersey*) And put on your jersey.

PAMELA (*moving to* L *of Louise*) Oh, phooey.

LOUISE. Darling, it's cold out.

PAMELA. It isn't really.

LOUISE. Pam, it's very cold. Now, do be sensible.

PAMELA. Mother, I can't put on any more—I'd just die.

LOUISE (*pushing the jersey into Pamela's hand; snapping*) Do as I say. Put on your jersey.

(LOUISE *turns abruptly, goes into the hall, then up the stairs to the schoolroom. She closes the living-room door behind her.* PAMELA *looks after her in surprise*)

PAMELA (*puzzled*) 'Bye.

FROST ON THE ROSE

By T. B. Morris

Lady Jane Grey, queen for nine days, has been accused of high treason, and Mary Tudor, her cousin, is crowned in her place. Elizabeth is Mary's young, impetuous half-sister.

SCENE—*The ante-room in the Tower of London.*
TIME—*The morning of 25th January 1554.*

MARY. I have sent an order to Sir John Brydges that I will see the Lady Jane here.

ELIZABETH (*rising*) Mary—you will never sign that child's death-warrant?

MARY. I pray God I never shall. But who can say what the folly of others may not do?

ELIZABETH. Folly?

MARY (*dryly*) You well know, sister, what that word means.

ELIZABETH. I? What mean you?

MARY. That you have not always been wise enough to keep your fingers from the fire.

ELIZABETH. Now before God I protest . . .

MARY (*interrupting*) Do not bring God's name into a perjury. I know well, Elizabeth, what part you have taken against me. And you should know that I am not a fool. One does not play hoodman-blind about the throne of England. You come riding to London to protest your loyalty, yet I am not sure that I should not have you, too, under lock and key.

ELIZABETH (*starting, between fear and anger*) Take my liberty—again?

MARY. Ay. Had our father found you in like case, you would have paid with more than your liberty.

(*There is a tense pause*)

(*She sighs*) Oh, there are still plots enough, and discontents. There are writings against the marriage I propose . . .

ELIZABETH (*interrupting, hotly*) The plots are all against your marriage, not against you. The people love you, but they will not have this Spanish Don Philip on the throne of England.

MARY (*angrily*) They shall have whom *I* will.

ELIZABETH. And they will not stomach the Inquisition here in London. Nor will they now acknowledge any Head of the Church other than the Sovereign of England.

35

MARY. His Holiness the Pope is God's Vicar on earth and the Head of the Church, here as elsewhere.

ELIZABETH. Your half-English blood, sister, has not given you a half-understanding of Englishmen. We are neither coerced nor compelled to any one faith or another. We worship as we choose.

MARY. Enough, sister! If there is heresy remaining, I shall burn it out.

ELIZABETH (*horrified*) Burn? Where is your kindness now?

MARY. Is it not kindness to burn the body that the soul may not burn?

ELIZABETH (*angrily*) Priests' talk!

MARY (*angrily*) Elizabeth! Have care o' your tongue.

ELIZABETH (*recovering, laughing*) Ah! Take my own advice given but now to Ellen. (*She moves to the steps of the chair and sits on them, looking up at Mary*) Oh, a fig for quarrelling! You are Queen and must go your own way—and never believe that I would stand in that way, or do you any hurt. We are sisters and have this much in common—that we have both suffered grievously for the sake of our mothers.

MARY (*stubbornly*) Ay. But my mother was a great princess and virtuous . . . (*She hesitates*)

(ELIZABETH *has grown tense and is about to explode again into anger. She controls herself, however*)

ELIZABETH (*lightly*) Well then, mine was brave and beautiful. (*She leaps up and dances to the window*) So what would you? (*She turns to Mary*) I protest, sister, I have no desire for your place. Give me a good horse and the clean air and English turf. (*She drops a curtsy*) I am your Grace's most loyal subject.

MARY (*slowly, not looking at Elizabeth*) I have been oft deceived. It is not easy for me to accept—oaths of allegiance.

ELIZABETH. Not even mine? The word of a princess and your sister?

MARY. Half-sister—and in that degree there is a whole sphere of difference. I tell you this, Elizabeth: I know of a certain plot of rebellion now ripening against me, and I bid you have care how far you may be embrangled in it. (*She is looking straight before her still*)

(ELIZABETH *is watching her tensely*)

You see that I love you well enough to warn you—for the sake of the two unhappy children we once were. (*She covers her face with her hands, wearily*)

ELIZABETH (*in a low voice full of sincerity*) I have no hand—nor ever had—in any plot against you. I have no mind towards so high and lonely a place as that you have. Give me life and love.

MARY (*looking at Elizabeth, wondering about her*) Lonely, you say—and love, you say? Then why do you deny me love and ease of my loneliness?

ELIZABETH. I do not.

MARY (*sharply*) You speak against the man I love.

ELIZABETH (*starting in surprise, moving down a few steps towards Mary*) The man you *love?* What? This Philip of Spain? But you have never seen him.

MARY (*taking a miniature from her breast*) I have his likeness—a noble likeness. (*She looks at the miniature lovingly, then replaces it*)

ELIZABETH (*disgusted*) Noble—faugh! A man at once cold and lecherous.

MARY (*starting to her feet in a rage*) Elizabeth!

ELIZABETH (*lost to caution*) A man whose amours are the scandal of Europe, and who smears them over with a sickly piety—calculating—sneering. Able enough in politics, I doubt not, but—oh, in God's truth, *he* would gain much by this marriage. But you—ah!

(MARY, *unable to bear more, darts to Elizabeth and stops her by striking her on the cheek.* ELIZABETH *cries out and starts back, her hand to her cheek*)

MARY (*passionately*) You—with your slut's behaviour—*would* see things thus. Love! You do not read the word as I read it.

ELIZABETH. I am no slut.

MARY (*cutting in*) You learned your picture of love with the late Lord of Sudeley.

ELIZABETH. Lies, lies, lies!

(*Flaming with rage, she advances on* MARY, *who starts back to the steps of the chair. Then* ELIZABETH'S *Tudor caution and strength again come to her aid. She controls herself and stands stiffly with her hands at her sides, breathing quickly with the great effort she is making*)

MARY (*shaken and ashamed*) Elizabeth! (*She drops on to the steps of the chair in a flood of tears*)

(ELIZABETH *recovers and laughs*)

ELIZABETH. Nay, sister! We're not a pair o' fishwives from Wapping. (*She goes to Mary, kneels and puts her arms about her*) Let us kiss and be friends again. Take the husband of your choosing, and God give you joy of him and a son for England. (*Her voice is warm, but her eyes are cold as she looks over the top of Mary's bent head, and her expression is one of contempt and hatred*)

MARY (*tearfully*) You are stronger than I. (*Wistfully*) A son! God grant me a son.

THE GLASS MENAGERIE

By Tennessee Williams

*Amanda Wingfield—a little woman of great but confused vitality, clinging
frantically to another time and place—has persuaded her son, Tom, to bring
home a gentleman caller for his sister, Laura, who is slightly crippled, one
leg being shorter than the other. The defect has left her nervous, very shy
and as fragile as a piece of her own glass collection.*

SCENE—*The Wingfield apartment, St. Louis.*
TIME—*Late 1920's.*

(AMANDA *crouches before Laura, adjusting the hem of the dress*)

AMANDA (*impatiently*) Why are you trembling?
LAURA. Mother, you've made me so nervous!
AMANDA. How have I made you nervous?
LAURA. By all this fuss! You make it seem so important.
AMANDA. I don't understand you, Laura. You couldn't be satis-
fied with just sitting home, and yet whenever I try to arrange some-
thing for you, you seem to resist it. (*She gets up*) Now take a look at
yourself. No, wait. Wait just a moment—I have an idea!
LAURA. What is it now?

(AMANDA *produces two powder-puffs which she wraps in handkerchiefs
and stuffs in Laura's bosom*)

LAURA. Mother, what are you doing?
AMANDA. They call them "Gay Deceivers"!
LAURA. I won't wear them!
AMANDA. You will!
LAURA. Why should I?
AMANDA. Because, to be painfully honest, your chest is flat.
LAURA. You make it seem like we were setting a trap.
AMANDA. All pretty girls are a trap, a pretty trap, and men expect
them to be! Now look at yourself, young lady. This is the prettiest
you will ever be. I've got to fix myself now. You're going to be sur-
prised by your mother's appearance.

(AMANDA *exits humming gaily.* LAURA *moves slowly to the long mirror
and stares solemnly at herself*)

AMANDA (*off stage*) It isn't dark enough yet.

(LAURA *turns slowly before the mirror with a troubled look*)

(*Laughing; off*) I'm going to show you something. I'm going to make a spectacular appearance.

LAURA. What is it, Mother?

AMANDA. Possess your soul in patience—you will see. Something I've resurrected from that old trunk. Styles haven't changed so terribly much after all . . .

(AMANDA *enters*)

Now just look at your mother. (*She wears a girlish frock of yellowed voile with a blue silk sash. She carries a bunch of jonquils; feverishly*) This is the dress in which I led the cotillion, won the cakewalk twice at Sunset Hill, wore one spring to the Governor's ball in Jackson. See how I sashayed around the ballroom, Laura? (*She raises her skirt and does a mincing step around the room*) I wore it on Sundays for my gentleman callers. I had it on the day I met your father . . . I had malaria fever all that spring. The change of climate from East Tennessee to the Delta—weakened resistance—I had a little temperature all the time not enough to be serious—just enough to make me restless and giddy. Invitations poured in—parties all over the Delta. "Stay in bed," said Mother, "you have fever." But I just wouldn't. I took quinine but kept on going, going. Evenings, dances. Afternoons, long, long rides. Picnics—lovely. So lovely, that country in May. All lacy with dogwood, literally flooded with jonquils. That was the spring I had the craze for jonquils. Jonquils became an absolute obsession. Mother said, "Honey, there's no more room for jonquils." And still I kept on bringing in more jonquils. Whenever, wherever I saw them, I'd say, "Stop. Stop. I see jonquils." I made the young men help me gather the jonquils. It was a joke. Amanda and her jonquils. Finally there were no more vases to hold them, every available space was filled with jonquils. No vases to hold them? All right, I'll hold them myself. And then I—met your father. Malaria fever and jonquils and then—this—boy . . . (*She switches on the rose-coloured lamp*) I hope they get here before it starts to rain. (*She places jonquils in a bowl on table*) I gave your brother a little extra change so he and Mr O'Connor could take the service car home.

LAURA (*with altered look*) What did you say his name was?

AMANDA. O'Connor.

LAURA. What is his first name?

AMANDA. I don't remember. Oh, yes, I do. It was—Jim.

(LAURA *sways slightly and catches hold of a chair*)

LAURA (*faintly*) Not—Jim.

AMANDA. Yes, that was it, it was Jim. I've never known a Jim that wasn't nice.

LAURA. Are you sure his name is Jim O'Connor?

AMANDA. Yes. Why?

LAURA. Is he the one that Tom used to know in high school?

AMANDA. He didn't say so. I think he just got to know him at the warehouse.

LAURA. There was a Jim O'Connor we both knew in high school—(*Then, with effort*) If that is the one that Tom is bringing to dinner—you'll have to excuse me, I won't come to the table.

AMANDA. What sort of nonsense is this?

LAURA. You asked me once if I'd ever liked a boy. Don't you remember I showed you this boy's picture?

AMANDA. You mean the boy you showed me in the year book?

LAURA. Yes, that boy.

AMANDA. Laura, Laura, were you in love with that boy?

LAURA. I don't know, Mother. All I know is I couldn't sit at the table if it was him.

AMANDA. It won't be him. It isn't the least bit likely. But whether it is or not, you will come to the table. You'll not be excused.

LAURA. I'll have to be, Mother.

AMANDA. I don't intend to humour your silliness, Laura. I've had too much from you and your brother, both. So just sit down and compose yourself till they come. Tom has forgotten his key so you'll have to let them in, when they arrive.

LAURA (*panicky*) Oh, Mother—*you* answer the door.

AMANDA (*lightly*) I'll be in the kitchen—busy.

LAURA. Oh, Mother, please answer the door, don't make me do it.

AMANDA (*crossing to the kitchenette*) I've got to fix the dressing for the salmon. Fuss, fuss—silliness. Over a gentleman caller.

LAURA *utters a low moan and turns off the lamp—sits stiffly on the edge of the sofa, knotting her fingers together.*

HEARTBREAK HOUSE

By George Bernard Shaw

Ellie Dunn, pretty, determined, has fallen in love with a man she knows as Marcus Darnley, but when it is revealed that he is Hector, husband of her benefactress, the scintillating and handsome Hesione Hushabye, she resolves to marry instead a rich, elderly man, Boss Mangan. (Mangan is asleep in a chair)

Scene—*A room built to resemble part of a ship in the country home of Captain Shotover, Mrs Hushabye's father.*
Time—*1919.*

ELLIE. Hesione: what the devil do you mean by making mischief with my father about Mangan?

Mrs Hushabye (*promptly losing her temper*) Don't you dare speak to me like that, you little minx. Remember that you are in my house.

ELLIE. Stuff! Why don't you mind your own business? What is it to you whether I choose to marry Mangan or not?

Mrs Hushabye. Do you suppose you can bully me, you miserable little matrimonial adventurer?

ELLIE. Every woman who hasn't any money is a matrimonial adventurer. It's easy for you to talk: you have never known what it is to want money; and you can pick up men as if they were daisies. I am poor and respectable . . .

Mrs Hushabye (*interrupting*) Ho! respectable! How did you pick up Mangan? How did you pick up my husband? You have the audacity to tell me that I am a—a—a . . .

ELLIE. A siren. So you are. You were born to lead men by the nose: if you weren't, Marcus would have waited for me, perhaps.

Mrs Hushabye (*suddenly melting and half laughing*) Oh, my poor Ellie, my pettikins, my unhappy darling! I am so sorry about Hector. But what can I do? It's not my fault: I'd give him to you if I could.

ELLIE. I don't blame you for that.

Mrs Hushabye. What a brute I was to quarrel with you and call you names! Do kiss me and say you're not angry with me.

ELLIE (*fiercely*) Oh, don't slop and gush and be sentimental. Don't you see that unless I can be hard—as hard as nails—I shall go mad. I don't care a damn about your calling me names: do you think a woman in my situation can feel a few hard words?

Mrs Hushabye. Poor little woman! Poor little situation!

ELLIE. I suppose you think you're being sympathetic. You are just foolish and stupid and selfish. You see me getting a smasher right in the face that kills a whole part of my life: the best part that can never come again; and you think you can help me over it by a little coaxing and kissing. When I want all the strength I can get to lean on: something iron, something stony, I don't care how cruel it is, you go all mush and want to slobber over me. I'm not angry; I'm not unfriendly; but for God's sake do pull yourself together; and don't think that because you're on velvet and always have been, women who are in hell can take it as easily as you.

MRS HUSHABYE (*shrugging her shoulders*) Very well. (*She sits down on the sofa in her old place*) But I warn you that when I am neither coaxing and kissing nor laughing, I am just wondering how much longer I can stand living in this cruel, damnable world. You object to the siren: well, I drop the siren. You want to rest your wounded bosom against a grindstone. Well, (*folding her arms*) here is the grindstone.

ELLIE (*sitting down beside her, appeased*) That's better: you really have the trick of falling in with everyone's mood; but you don't understand, because you are not the sort of woman for whom there is only one man and only one chance.

MRS HUSHABYE. I certainly don't understand how your marrying that object—(*indicating Mangan*) will console you for not being able to marry Hector.

ELLIE. Perhaps you don't understand why I was quite a nice girl this morning, and am now neither a girl nor particularly nice.

MRS HUSHABYE. Oh, yes, I do. It's because you have made up your mind to do something despicable and wicked.

ELLIE. I don't think so, Hesione. I must make the best of my ruined house.

MRS HUSHABYE. Pooh! You'll get over it. Your house isn't ruined.

ELLIE. Of course I shall get over it. You don't suppose I'm going to sit down and die of a broken heart, I hope, or be an old maid living on a pittance from the Sick and Indigent Roomkeepers' Association. But my heart is broken, all the same. What I mean by that is that I know that what has happened to me with Marcus will not happen to me ever again. In the world for me there is Marcus and a lot of other men of whom one is just the same as another. Well, if I can't have love, that's no reason why I should have poverty. If Mangan has nothing else, he has money.

MRS HUSHABYE. And are there no young men with money?

ELLIE. Not within my reach. Besides, a young man would have the right to expect love from me, and would perhaps leave me when he found I could not give it to him. Rich young men can get rid of their wives, you know, pretty cheaply. But this object, as you call him, can expect nothing more from me than I am prepared to give him.

MRS HUSHABYE. He will be your owner, remember. If he buys

you, he will make the bargain pay him and not you. Ask your father.

ELLIE (*rising and strolling to the chair to contemplate their subject*) You need not trouble on that score, Hesione. I have more to give Boss Mangan than he has to give me: it is I who am buying him, and at a pretty good price too, I think. Women are better at that sort of bargain than men. I have taken the Boss's measure; and ten Boss Mangans shall not prevent me doing far more as I please as his wife than I have ever been able to do as a poor girl. (*Stooping to the recumbent figure*) Shall they, Boss? I think not. (*She passes on to the drawing-table, and leans against the end of it, facing the windows*) I shall not have to spend most of my time wondering how long my gloves will last, anyhow.

MRS HUSHABYE (*rising superbly*) Ellie: you are a wicked sordid little beast. And to think that I actually condescended to fascinate that creature there to save you from him! Well, let me tell you this: if you make this disgusting match, you will never see Hector again if I can help it.

ELLIE (*unmoved*) I nailed Mangan by telling him that if he did not marry me he should never see you again. (*She lifts herself on her wrists and seats herself on the end of the table*)

MRS HUSHABYE (*recoiling*) Oh!

ELLIE. So you see I am not unprepared for your playing that trump against me. Well, you just try it: that's all. I should have made a man of Marcus, not a household pet.

MRS HUSHABYE (*flaming*) You dare!

ELLIE (*looking almost dangerous*) Set him thinking about me if you dare.

MRS HUSHABYE. Well, of all the impudent little fiends I ever met! Hector says there is a certain point at which the only answer you can give to a man who breaks all the rules is to knock him down. What would you say if I were to box your ears?

ELLIE (*calmly*) I should pull your hair.

MRS HUSHABYE (*mischievously*) That wouldn't hurt me. Perhaps it comes off at night.

ELLIE (*so taken aback that she drops off the table and runs to her*) Oh, you don't mean to say, Hesione, that your beautiful black hair is false?

MRS HUSHABYE (*patting it*) Don't tell Hector. He believes in it.

ELLIE (*groaning*) Oh! Even the hair that ensnared him false! Everything false!

MRS HUSHABYE. Pull it and try. Other women can snare men in their hair; but I can swing a baby on mine. Aha! you can't do that, Goldylocks.

ELLIE (*heartbroken*) No. You have stolen my babies.

MRS HUSHABYE. Pettikins: don't make me cry. You know, what you said about my making a household pet of him is a little true, Perhaps he ought to have waited for you. Would any other woman on earth forgive you?

ELLIE. Oh, what right had you to take him all for yourself! (*Pulling herself together*) There! You couldn't help it: neither of us could help it. He couldn't help it. No: don't say anything more: I can't bear it. Let us wake the object.

HEDDA GABLER

By Henrik Ibsen

Translated by Una Ellis-Fermor

Hedda, a beautiful but cold woman, recently married to historian Jorgen Tesman, has in the past been closely involved with Ejlert Lovberg, a writer. Mrs Elvsted, about twenty-seven, small, pretty and vulnerable, is attracted to Ejlert and is trying to help him.

Scene—*The drawing-room of Jorgen Tesman's villa.*
Time—*1890.*

Hedda (*goes up to Mrs Elvsted and says softly*) That's right. Now we've killed two birds with one stone.

Mrs Elvsted. How do you mean?

Hedda. Didn't you realize I wanted to get rid of him?

Mrs Elvsted. Yes, to write his letter.

Hedda. And also so that I could talk to you alone.

Mrs Elvsted (*confused*) About this business?

Hedda. Exactly. About that.

Mrs Elvsted (*alarmed*) But there isn't anything more, Mrs Tesman! Nothing at all!

Hedda. Oh, yes, there is, now. There's a lot more. That much I do realize. Come over here, and we'll sit and be cosy and friendly together. (*She pushes Mrs Elvsted into the easy-chair by the stove and sits on one of the stools herself*)

Mrs Elvsted (*looking anxiously at her watch*) But my dear Mrs Tesman, I really meant to go now.

Hedda. Oh, surely there's no hurry. Now then, suppose you tell me a little about what your home's like.

Mrs Elvsted. But that's the last thing in the world I wanted to talk about!

Hedda. Not to me, my dear? After all, we were at school together.

Mrs Elvsted. Yes, but you were a class above me. How dreadfully frightened of you I was in those days!

Hedda. Were you frightened of me?

Mrs Elvsted. Yes. Dreadfully frightened. Because when we met on the stairs you always used to pull my hair.

Hedda. No, *did* I?

Mrs Elvsted. Yes, and once you said you would burn it off.

Hedda. Oh, that was only silly talk, you know.

Mrs Elvsted. Yes, but I was so stupid in those days. And since then, anyhow, we have drifted such a long, long way apart. Our circles were so entirely different.

HEDDA. Well, then, we'll see if we can come together again. Now, look here. When we were at school we used to talk like real close friends and call each other by our Christian names.

MRS ELVSTED. Oh, no, you're making quite a mistake.

HEDDA. I certainly am *not*. I remember it perfectly well. So we are going to tell each other everything, as we did in the old days. (*Moving nearer with her stool*) There we are! (*Kissing her cheek*) Now you're to talk to me like a real friend and call me "Hedda".

MRS ELVSTED (*clasping and patting her hands*) All this goodness and kindness—it's not a bit what I'm used to.

HEDDA. There, there, there! And I'm going to treat *you* like a friend, as I did before, and call you my dear Thora.

MRS ELVSTED. My name's Thea.

HEDDA. Yes, of course. Of course. I meant Thea. (*Looking sympathetically at her*) So you're not used to much goodness or kindness, aren't you, Thea? Not in your own home?

MRS ELVSTED. Ah, if I *had* a home! But I haven't one. Never have had. . . .

HEDDA (*looking at her a moment*) I rather thought it must be something of that sort.

MRS ELVSTED (*gazing helplessly in front of her*) Yes. Yes. Yes.

HEDDA. I can't quite remember now, but wasn't it as housekeeper that you went up there in the beginning—to the District Magistrate's?

MRS ELVSTED. Actually it was to have been as governess. But his wife—his late wife—was an invalid and was ill in bed most of the time. So I had to take charge of the house too.

HEDDA. But then, in the end, you became the mistress of the house.

MRS ELVSTED (*drearily*) Yes, I did.

HEDDA. Let me see. . . . About how long ago is it now?

MRS ELVSTED. Since I was married?

HEDDA. Yes.

MRS ELVSTED. It's five years ago now.

HEDDA. Yes, of course. It must be that.

MRS ELVSTED. Ah! Those five years—or rather the last two or three. Oh, if you could only imagine, Mrs Tesman . . .

HEDDA (*giving her a little slap on the hand*) Mrs Tesman! Come, Thea!

MRS ELVSTED. Oh, yes; I will try! Yes, Hedda, if you had any idea—if you understood . . .

HEDDA (*casually*) Ejlert Lövborg was up there too for three years or so, I believe?

MRS ELVSTED (*looking at her doubtfully*) Ejlert Lövborg? Why yes. He was.

HEDDA. Did you know him already? From the old days in town?

MRS ELVSTED. Hardly at all. Well, I mean—by name, of course.

HEDDA. But when you were up there—then, he used to visit you and your husband?

MRS ELVSTED. Yes, he came over to us every day. You see, he was giving the children lessons. Because, in the long run, I couldn't manage it all myself.

HEDDA. No, I should think not. And your husband? I suppose he is often away from home?

MRS ELVSTED. Yes. You see, Mrs—er—you see, Hedda, being District Magistrate he's always having to go out on circuit.

HEDDA (*leaning against the arm of the chair*) Thea, my poor little Thea. Now you're going to tell me all about it. Just how things are.

MRS ELVSTED. Very well. You ask me about it, then.

HEDDA. What is your husband really like, Thea? You know what I mean—in everyday life? Is he nice to you?

MRS ELVSTED (*evasively*) He's quite sure himself that he does everything for the best.

HEDDA. Only, it seems to me, he must be much too old for you. More than twenty years older, surely?

MRS ELVSTED (*irritably*) Yes, there's that too. What with one thing and another, I'm miserable with him. We haven't an idea in common, he and I. Not a thing in the world.

HEDDA. But isn't he fond of you, all the same? I mean, in his own way?

MRS ELVSTED. Oh, I don't know *what* he feels. I think I'm just useful to him. After all, it doesn't cost much to keep me. I'm cheap.

HEDDA. That's silly of you.

MRS ELVSTED (*shaking her head*) It can't be any different. Not with him. He isn't really fond of anyone but himself. And perhaps the children—a little.

HEDDA. And of Ejlert Lövborg, Thea.

MRS ELVSTED (*looking at her*) Of Ejlert Lövborg? What makes you think that?

HEDDA. But, my dear—it seems to me, when he sends you all the way into town after him. . . . (*Smiling almost imperceptibly*) And besides, you said so yourself to my husband.

MRS ELVSTED (*with a nervous start*) What? Oh, yes, so I did. (*Breaking out, but in a lowered voice*) No. I might as well tell you now as later. It'll all come out, anyway.

HEDDA. But, my dear Thea . . .

MRS ELVSTED. Well, to be quite frank, my husband had no idea I was coming.

HEDDA. *What!* Didn't your husband know about it?

MRS ELVSTED. No, of course not. And, anyway, he wasn't at home. He was away too. Oh, I couldn't stand it any longer, Hedda! It was simply impossible. I should have been absolutely alone up there in future.

HEDDA. Well? So then?

MRS ELVSTED. So I packed up some of my things, you see—the ones I needed most. Very quietly, of course. And so I left the place.

HEDDA. Just like that? Nothing more?

MRS ELVSTED. No. . . . And then I took the train straight in to town.

HEDDA. But, my dear, precious child! How did you dare risk it?

MRS ELVSTED (*getting up and moving across the room*) Well, what on earth could I do?

HEDDA. But what do you think your husband will say when you go back again?

MRS ELVSTED (*by the table, looking at her*) Back there, to him?

HEDDA. Yes, of course. What then?

MRS ELVSTED. I'm never going back there to him.

HEDDA (*getting up and going nearer to her*) Then you've left in real earnest, for good and all?

MRS ELVSTED. Yes. There didn't seem to be anything else for me to do.

HEDDA. And then—your doing it quite openly!

MRS ELVSTED. Oh, you can't keep that kind of thing secret, in any case.

HEDDA. But, Thea, what do you think people will say about you?

MRS ELVSTED. Heaven knows, they must say what they like. (*Sitting down on the sofa wearily and sadly*) I have only done what I *had* to do.

HEDDA (*after a short silence*) What do you mean to do now? What kind of job are you going to get?

MRS ELVSTED. I don't know yet. I only know that I must live here, where Ejlert Lövborg lives. That is, if I *must* live. . . .

HEDDA (*moves a chair from the table, sits beside her and strokes her hands*) Thea, my dear, how did it happen? This—this friendship between you and Ejlert Lövborg?

MRS ELVSTED. Oh, it happened by degrees, somehow. I came to have some kind of power over him.

HEDDA. Indeed? And then?

MRS ELVSTED. He gave up his old habits. Not because I asked him to. I never dared do that. But of course he noticed I didn't like that kind of thing. And so he left off.

HEDDA (*masking an involuntary sneer*) In fact, you've what they call "reclaimed him", you have, little Thea.

MRS ELVSTED. Yes, At least, he says so himself. And he, for his part, has made me into a real human being! Taught me to think. . . . and to understand . . . one thing after another.

HEDDA. Perhaps he gave *you* lessons, too, did he?

MRS ELVSTED. No, not exactly lessons. . . . But he used to talk to me about such endless numbers of things. And then came the glorious, happy moment when I began to share his work! When he let me help him.

HEDDA. And you did, did you?

MRS ELVSTED. Yes. When he was writing anything, we always had to work at it together.

HEDDA. I see. Like two good comrades.

MRS ELVSTED (*eagerly*) Comrades! Why, Hedda, that's just what he called it! Oh, I ought to feel so perfectly happy. But I can't, though. Because I really don't know whether it will last.

HEDDA. Aren't you surer of him than that?

MRS ELVSTED (*drearily*) There's the shadow of a woman standing between Ejlert Lövborg and me.

HEDDA (*looking intently at her*) Who can that be?

MRS ELVSTED. I don't know. Someone or other from—from his past. Someone he's never really forgotten.

HEDDA. What has he said . . . about it?

MRS ELVSTED. He only touched on it once—and quite vaguely.

HEDDA. Oh. And what did he say, then?

MRS ELVSTED. He said that when they parted she wanted to shoot him with a pistol.

HEDDA (*cold and controlled*) How absurd! People don't do that kind of thing here.

MRS ELVSTED. No. And that's why I thought it must be that red-haired singer that he once . . .

HEDDA. Yes, that may be.

MRS ELVSTED. Because I remember people used to talk about her carrying loaded firearms.

HEDDA. Oh well, then, it's obviously she.

MRS ELVSTED (*wringing her hands*) Yes, but just think, Hedda, now I hear that singer—she's in town again! Oh, I'm simply desperate!

HEDDA (*glancing towards the inner room*) Sh! Here comes my husband. (*Getting up and whispering*) Thea, all this must be between our two selves.

MRS ELVSTED (*springing up*) Why, yes! For heaven's sake!

I CAPTURE THE CASTLE

By DODIE SMITH

Living in an old castle with an eccentric writer father and a glamorous, bizarre stepmother, loses its appeal for pretty eighteen-year-old Rose, who thinks that marriage to a rich American is a solution to poverty and bohemian living. Cassandra, her imaginative, intelligent younger sister, tells their story through her diary.

SCENE—*The kitchen of an old house grafted on to the ruins of Godsend Castle, Suffolk.*

TIME—*The middle nineteen-thirties.*

CASSANDRA. I won't try to find out if Rose cares for him—what's the use? And I mustn't, I mustn't let her know about me.

(ROSE *enters* R. CASSANDRA *turns a brilliant smile on her*)

ROSE (*crossing up* C) Topaz is actually dancing across the court-yard. She gets more bogus every day.

CASSANDRA. Yet somehow she's genuine, too. How mixed people are. How mixed and nice.

(ROSE *takes a spray of honeysuckle out of her button-hole*)

Oh, honeysuckle!

ROSE. Messy stuff. (*She moves to the window up* L) Simon stopped the car to gather me some. (*She throws the honeysuckle out of the window with a contemptuous gesture*)

CASSANDRA (*crossing up* LC) Rose! You don't love him.

ROSE (*ironically*) No. Pity, isn't it?

CASSANDRA. Why did you lie to me the night you got engaged?

ROSE. I didn't. When he kissed me it was—well, exciting. I thought that meant I was in love. (*She moves to the chair* L *of the table and sits*) You wouldn't understand. You're too young.

CASSANDRA (*moving to* L *of Rose*) I understand, all right. How long have you known?

ROSE. For ages. But it's got worse since I went to London—he's with me so much more there. Every minute we're together I can feel him *asking* for love. He somehow links it with everything—if it's a lovely day or we see anything beautiful. Oh, it's such a comfort to talk to you.

CASSANDRA (*holding Rose's hands*) Poor Rose. Would you like me to tell him for you?

ROSE. Tell him? (*She turns away*) Oh, I'm still going to marry him.

CASSANDRA (*crossing above the table to* C) You are not. You're not going to do anything so wicked.

ROSE. Why is it suddenly wicked? You helped me to get him long before you thought I was in love with him.

CASSANDRA (*turning away*) I didn't understand. It was just fun—like something in a book. It wasn't real.

ROSE. Well, it's real enough now.

CASSANDRA (*leaning on the table*) You can't do it, Rose—not just for clothes and jewellery.

ROSE. You talk as if I'm doing it all for myself. Do you know what my last thought has been, night after night? "At least they've had enough to eat at the castle today." And I've thought of you more than anyone—(*she reaches out to Cassandra's hands*) of all I'm going to do for you.

CASSANDRA (*drawing away to* R) Then you can stop thinking—because I won't take anything from you. And you can stop pretending to be noble. You're going to wreck his whole life.

(ROSE *gives her a swift look of astonished understanding*)

When he's the most wonderful person who ever lived . . . (*She breaks off, seeing Rose's expression*)

ROSE (*rising*) You're in love with him yourself. (*She crosses to Cassandra and holds her arms. Very much distressed*) Oh, no! Darling, listen. I swear I'd give him up if he'd marry you instead. I'd be glad to because he'd still go on helping us. I don't want a lot of luxury—but I won't let us all go back to such hideous poverty. And we'd have to if I gave him up, because he'd never fall in love with you. He thinks of you as a little girl.

CASSANDRA. What he thinks of me's got nothing to do with it. It's *him* I'm thinking of.

ROSE. Do you realize what would happen if I broke the engagement? He'd let Scoatney Hall to the Fox-Cottons and go back to America with Neil. How would you like that?

CASSANDRA. You're not going to marry him without loving him.

ROSE. Don't you know he'd rather have me that way than not at all?

(*A motor horn is heard off* R)

There's the car back. (*She crosses to* L *of the table*) We'll talk again.

(CASSANDRA *crosses to the easy chair*)

I'm supposed to be staying at Scoatney tonight, but I'll say I want to be with you. We'll try to help each other.

CASSANDRA. If you come back here, I won't speak to you. And I'm not coming to Scoatney. I'm not going to watch you show your power over him.

ROSE. But you must come. What'll they think if you don't?

CASSANDRA. Tell them I have a headache.

ROSE. If you knew how wretched I am . . .

CASSANDRA. Go and make a list of your trousseau—that'll cheer you up. You grasping little cheat.

ROSE. You're failing me just when I need you most.

I REMEMBER MAMA

By John van Druten

Katrin Hanson, eldest daughter of humble Norwegians, who have settled in San Francisco, has always wanted to be a writer, but it is through Mama's indomitable personality that she finally achieves her aim.

Scene—*Katrin's attic room.*
Time—*1910.*

KATRIN. When mama came back, I was sitting with my diary, which I called my Journal now, writing a Tragic Farewell to my Art. It was very seldom that mama came to the attic, thinking that a writer needed privacy, and I was surprised to see her standing in the doorway. (*She looks up*)

(MAMA *has entered* c *through the* TABS *and is standing on the steps*)

Mama!

MAMA. You are busy, Katrin?

KATRIN (*jumping up*) No, of course not. Come in.

MAMA (*coming down*) I like to talk to you.

KATRIN. Yes, of course.

MAMA (*seating herself at the desk*) You are writing?

KATRIN (*on the steps*) No. I told you, that's all over.

MAMA. That is what I want to talk to you about.

KATRIN. It's all right, Mama. Really, it's all right. I was planning to tear up all my stories this afternoon, only I couldn't find half of them.

MAMA. They are here.

KATRIN. Did *you* take them? What for?

MAMA. Katrin, I have been to see Miss Moorhead.

KATRIN. Who's Miss . . . ? You don't mean Florence Dana Moorhead?

(MAMA *nods*)

You don't mean . . . (*She comes down to her*) Mama, you don't mean you took her my stories?

MAMA. She read five of them. I was two hours with her. We have glass of sherry. Two glass of sherry.

KATRIN. What—what did she say about them?

MAMA (*quietly*) She say they are not good.

KATRIN (*turning away*) Well, I knew that. It was hardly worth your going to all that trouble just to be told that.

MAMA. She say more. Will you listen, Katrin?

KATRIN (*trying to be gracious*) Sure. Sure. I'll listen.

MAMA. I will try and remember. She say you write now only because of what you have read in other books, and that no-one can write good until they have felt what they write about. That for years she write bad stories about people in the olden times, until one day she remember something that happen in her own town—something that only she could know and understand—and she feels she must tell it . . . and that is how she write her first good story. She say you must write more of things you know . . .

KATRIN. That's what my teacher always told me at school.

MAMA. Maybe your teacher was right. I do not know if I explain good what Miss Moorhead means, but while she talks I think I understand. Your story about the painter who is blind—that is because . . . forgive me if I speak plain, my Katrin, but it is important to you . . . because you are the dramatic one, as papa has said . . . and you think it would feel good to be a painter and be blind and not complain. But never have you imagined how it would really be. Is true?

KATRIN (*subdued*) Yes, I—I guess it's true.

MAMA. But she say you are to go on writing. That you have the gift.

(KATRIN *turns back to her, suddenly aglow*)

And that when you have written story that is real and true . . . then you send it to someone whose name she give me. (*She fumbles for a piece of paper*) It is her—agent—and say she recommended you. Here. No, that is recipe she give me for goulash as her grandmother make it . . . here. (*She hands over the paper*) It helps, Katrin, what I have told you?

KATRIN (*subdued again*) Yes, I—I guess it helps. Some. But what have *I* got to write about? I haven't seen anything, or been anywhere.

MAMA. Could you write about San Francisco, maybe? Is fine city. Miss Moorhead write about her home town.

KATRIN. Yes, I know. But you've got to have a central character or something. She writes about her grandfather—he was a wonderful old man.

MAMA. Could you maybe write about papa?

KATRIN. Papa?

MAMA. Papa is fine man. Is wonderful man.

KATRIN. Yes, I know, but . . .

MAMA (*rising*) I must go fix supper. Is late. Papa will be home. (*She goes up the steps to the* TABS, *and then turns back*) I like you should write about papa.

(*She exits through the* TABS)

KATRIN (*going back to her seat behind the desk*) Papa. Yes, but what's he ever done? What's ever happened to him? What's ever happened to *any* of us? Except always being poor and having illness, like the time when Dagmar went to hospital and mama . . . (*The idea hits her like a flash*) Oh—oh . . . (*Pause—then she becomes the Katrin of today*) And that was how it was born—suddenly in a flash—the story of "Mama and the Hospital"—the first of all the stories. I wrote it—oh, quite soon after that. I didn't tell mama or any of them. But I sent it to Miss Moorhead's agent. It was a long time before I heard anything. And then one evening the letter came. (*She takes an envelope from the desk in front of her*) For a moment I couldn't believe it. Then I went rushing into the kitchen, shouting . . . (*She rises from the desk, taking some papers with her, and rushes up the steps*) Mama. Mama.

(*The* TABS *open on the kitchen and the family tableau.* MAMA *is seated* R *of the table with* CHRISTINE *standing behind her.* PAPA *is seated* L *of the table.* NELS *is seated on the chest.* DAGMAR *is not present.* KATRIN *comes rushing in, up the steps. The* R *turntable revolves out as soon as she has left it*)

MAMA . . . Mama . . . I've sold a story!

MAMA. A story?

KATRIN. Yes. I've got a letter from the agent—with a cheque for—(*gasping*) five hundred dollars!

THE LIVING ROOM

By Graham Greene

Rose Pemberton, a girl of twenty, has fallen in love with Michael Dennis, a middle-aged man appointed her guardian. This meeting with Michael's unhappy, neurotic wife finally breaks Rose.

Scene—*The living-room in a house in Holland Park, London.*
Period—*Modern.*

Mrs Dennis. Is Michael here?

Rose. No. Did you expect him to be?

Mrs Dennis. He said he was at a lecture, but I never know now. You're Rose, aren't you?

Rose. You're his wife, aren't you?

Mrs Dennis. I read one of your letters. It fell out of his dressing-gown pocket.

Rose. Yes?

Mrs Dennis. He's always been silly that way—keeping letters.

Rose. Is that what you've come to tell me? Was it worth climbing all those stairs?

Mrs Dennis (*maliciously*) I thought your letter so touching. You trust him so much.

Rose. Yes. I do.

Mrs Dennis. You shouldn't, you know, but of course you can't know, he wouldn't tell you. But there's always been trouble with his students. Reading Freud together, I suppose. The third year we were married—just after our baby died—I could have divorced him.

Rose. Why didn't you?

Mrs Dennis (*fiercely*) Because he's happier with me. He'll always be happier with me. I'd forgive him anything. Would you?

Rose. No. Because I love him. I wouldn't want to hold him prisoner with forgiveness. I wouldn't want to hold him a minute if he wanted to be somewhere else.

Mrs Dennis. He only *thinks* that.

Rose. He has a right to think. He has a right to think wrong.

Mrs Dennis. If he really loved you, he'd have left me.

Rose. He meant to. Three weeks ago.

Mrs Dennis. But he's still here.

Rose. Because I wouldn't go.

Mrs Dennis. Why?

Rose. I was caught like him. By pity (*savagely*) He pities you.

Mrs Dennis (*maliciously*) It didn't feel like pity—last night.

56

Rose (*crying out in pain*) I don't believe you.

Mrs Dennis. If I'm ready to share him, what right . . .

Rose. You're lying. You know you are lying. What have you come here for? You're just lying to break me. You're wicked.

Mrs Dennis. Wicked's an odd word from you. I *am* his wife.

Rose. You can stay his wife. I only want to be his mistress.

(Mrs Dennis *suddenly crumbles. She drops into a chair and begins to weep.* Rose *watches her for a moment, but she cannot remain indifferent*).

I'm sorry. (*With a gesture of despair*) Oh, it's all such a mess.

Mrs Dennis. Please don't take him away.

Rose. What can I do? I love him. I love him terribly.

Mrs Dennis. But I love him too. I only want him near me still. It doesn't hurt you.

Rose (*bitterly*) Doesn't it?

Mrs Dennis. I was lying. We haven't—been together like that for years.

Rose. Oh, love isn't all making love. I'd sometimes give that up, to be together. At meals. Come into a house where he is. Sit silent with a book in the same room.

Mrs Dennis (*hysterically*) When are you going? I know you are planning to go. Don't torture me. Tell me.

Rose. I don't know.

Mrs Dennis. You're young. You can find any number of men. Please let him alone. (*Spacing her words*) I can't live without him.

(Rose *watches her hysteria grow. She is trapped and horrified*)

I'll die if he leaves me. I'll kill myself.

Rose. No. No. You never will.

Mrs Dennis. I will. I know what you're thinking—after that, I could marry him.

Rose. Please . . .

Mrs Dennis. Go away from him. Please. Go somewhere he won't find you. You're young. You'll get over it. The young always do.

Rose. But I don't want to get over it.

Mrs Dennis. I'm ill. Can't you wait? Just wait six months and see. Six months isn't long. (*With almost a cry*) You haven't any right to hurt me like this. (*She gets up and comes across the floor to Rose*) No right. (*Suddenly she strikes Rose in the face, but immediately she has struck she goes down on her knees and starts beating the table with her fists*) You made me do that. You made me. I want to die. I want to die. I want to die.

(Rose *stands helplessly above her as* Mrs Dennis *beats the table. She doesn't know what to do*)

He wants me to die too. You all want me to die.

Rose. No. No. (*In a moan of despair*) We only want to be happy.

Mrs Dennis. If he runs away, I shall go mad. (*She gets clumsily to her feet. The paroxysm is over. She sits down in a chair again*) Please will you get me some water?

(ROSE *goes to the closet door. As she enters the closet,* MRS DENNIS *hurriedly gets up and finds her bag which she had laid on the table. A tap runs. She takes a bottle out of her bag and unscrews the top. As* ROSE *comes in again she conceals the bottle in her palm. She takes the glass of water*)

MRS DENNIS. Could you turn out that light, dear? It's so strong.

(ROSE *turns away to find the switch.* MRS DENNIS *begins to pour some tablets into her hand. She does it slowly with the obvious purpose that she shall be seen when* ROSE *turns. When* ROSE *sees what she is at, she runs to her and snatches the bottle which she throws into a corner of the room*)

(*Hysterically*) Why did you do that? I can buy more.

ROSE. Buy them then. You're just blackmailing me. (*She hears the sound of feet coming rapidly up the stairs and runs to the door*) Michael, for God's sake. *Michael!*

LOOK BACK IN ANGER

By John Osborne

The self-pity, pride, rudeness and sometimes, cruelty of Jimmy Porter, drive his attractive, sensitive wife to leave him. After a miscarriage, she returns to their flat and finds that her prudish actress friend, Helena, who had formerly loathed and disapproved of Jimmy, is having an affair with him.

Scene—*The Porters' one-room flat in a large midland town.*
Period—*Modern.*

> Helena *is standing* l *of the table, pouring out a cup of tea.* Alison *is sitting on the armchair* r. *She bends down and picks up Jimmy's pipe. Then she scoops up a little pile of ash from the floor, and drops it in the ashtray on the arm of the chair.*

ALISON. He still smokes this foul old stuff. I used to hate it at first, but you get used to it.

HELENA. Yes.

ALISON. I went to the pictures last week, and some old man was smoking it in front, a few rows away. I actually got up, and sat right behind him.

HELENA (*coming down with a cup of tea*) Here, have this. It usually seems to help.

ALISON (*taking it*) Thanks.

HELENA. Are you sure you feel all right now?

ALISON (*nods*) It was just—oh, everything. It's my own fault—entirely. I must be mad, coming here like this. I'm sorry, Helena.

HELENA. Why should you be sorry—you of all people?

ALISON. Because it was unfair and cruel of me to come back. I'm afraid a sense of timing is one of the things I seem to have learnt from Jimmy. But it's something that can be in very bad taste. (*Sips her tea*) So many times, I've just managed to stop myself coming here —right at the last moment. Even today, when I went to the booking office at St. Pancras, it was like a charade, and I never believed that I'd let myself walk on to the train. And when I was on it, I got into a panic. I felt like a criminal. I told myself I'd turn round at the other end, and come straight back. I couldn't even believe that this place existed any more. But once I got here, there was nothing I could do. I had to convince myself that everything I remembered about this place had really happened to me once. (*She lowers her cup, and her foot plays with the newspaper on the floor*) How many times in these past few months I've thought of the evenings we used to spend here in this room. Suspended and rather remote. You make a good cup of tea.

HELENA (*sitting* L *of the table*) Something Jimmy taught *me*.

ALISON (*covering her face*) Oh, why am I here! You must all wish me a thousand miles away!

HELENA. I don't wish anything of the kind. You've more right to be here than I.

ALISON. Oh, Helena, don't bring out the book of rules . . .

HELENA. You are his wife, aren't you? Whatever I have done, I've never been able to forget that fact. You have all the rights . . .

ALISON. Helena—even I gave up believing in the divine rights of marriage long ago. Even before I met Jimmy. They've got something different now—constitutional monarchy. You are where you are by consent. And if you start trying any strong arm stuff, you're out. And I'm out.

HELENA. Is that something you learnt from him?

ALISON. Don't make me feel like a blackmailer or something, please! I've done something foolish, and rather vulgar in coming here tonight. I regret it, and I detest myself for doing it. But I did not come here in order to gain anything. Whatever it was—hysteria or just macabre curiosity, I'd certainly no intention of making any kind of breach between you and Jimmy. You must believe that.

HELENA. Oh, I believe it all right. That's why everything seems more wrong and terrible than ever. You didn't even reproach me. You should have been outraged, but you weren't. (*She leans back, as if she wanted to draw back from herself*) I feel so—ashamed.

ALISON. You talk as though he were something you'd swindled me out of . . .

HELENA (*fiercely*) And you talk as if he were a book or something you pass around to anyone who happens to want it for five minutes. What's the matter with you? You sound as though you were quoting *him* all the time. I thought you told me once you couldn't bring yourself to believe in him.

ALISON. I don't think I ever believed in your way either.

HELENA. At least, I still believe in right and wrong! Not even the months in this madhouse have stopped me doing that. Even though everything I have done is wrong, at least I have known it was wrong.

ALISON. You loved him, didn't you? That's what you wrote, and told me.

HELENA. And it was true.

ALISON. It was pretty difficult to believe at the time. I couldn't understand it.

HELENA. I could hardly believe it myself.

ALISON. Afterwards, it wasn't quite so difficult. You used to say some pretty harsh things about him. Not that I was sorry to hear them—they were rather comforting then. But you even shocked me sometimes

HELENA. Do you know—I have discovered what is wrong with Jimmy? It's very simple really. He was born out of his time.

ALISON. Yes. I know.

HELENA. There's no place for people like that any longer—in sex, or politics, or anything. That's why he's so futile. Sometimes, when I listen to him, I feel he thinks he's still in the middle of the French Revolution. And that's where he ought to be, of course. He doesn't know where he is, or where he's going. He'll never do anything, and he'll never amount to anything.

ALISON. I suppose he's what you'd call an Eminent Victorian. Slightly comic—in a way . . . We seem to have had this conversation before.

HELENA. Yes, I remember everything you said about him. It horrified me. I couldn't believe that you could have married someone like that. Alison—it's all over between Jimmy and me. I can see it now. I've got to get out. No—listen to me. When I saw you standing there tonight, I knew that it was all utterly wrong. That I didn't believe in any of this, and not Jimmy or you or anyone could make me believe otherwise. (*Rising*) How could I have ever thought I could get away with it! He wants one world and I want another, and lying in that bed won't ever change it! I believe in good and evil, and I don't have to apologize for that. It's quite a modern, scientific belief now, so they tell me. And, by everything I have ever believed in, or wanted, what I have been doing is wrong and evil.

ALISON. Helena—you're not going to leave him?

HELENA. Yes, I am. (*Before Alison can interrupt, she goes on*) Oh, I'm not stepping aside to let you come back. You can do what you like. Frankly, I think you'd be a fool—but that's your business. I think I've given you enough advice.

· ALISON. But h—he'll have no one.

HELENA. Oh, my dear, he'll find somebody. He'll probably hold court here like one of the Renaissance Popes. Oh, I know I'm throwing the book of rules at you, as you call it, but, believe me, you're never going to be happy without it. I tried throwing it away all these months, but I know now it just doesn't work. When you came in at that door, ill and tired and hurt, it was all over for me. You see —I didn't know about the baby. It was such a shock. It's like a judgement on us.

ALISON. You saw me, and I had to tell you what had happened. I lost the child. It's a simple fact. There is no judgement, there's no blame . . .

HELENA. Maybe not. But I feel it just the same.

ALISON. But don't you see? It isn't logical!

HELENA. No, it isn't. (*Calmly*) But I know it's right.

HELENA. Do you think so?

ALISON. Maybe you're not the right one for him—we're neither of us right . . .

HELENA (*moving up stage*) Oh, why doesn't he stop that damned noise!

ALISON. He wants something quite different from us. What it is exactly I don't know—a kind of cross between a mother and a Greek courtesan, a henchwoman, a mixture of Cleopatra and Boswell. But give him a little longer . . .

HELENA (*wrenching the door open*) Please! Will you stop that. I can't think!

(*There is a slight pause, and the trumpet goes on. She puts her hands to her head*)

Jimmy, for God's sake!

(*It stops*)

Jimmy, I want to speak to you.

JIMMY (*off*) Is your friend still with you?

HELENA. Oh, don't be an idiot, and come in here!

ALISON (*rising*) He doesn't want to see me.

HELENA. Stay where you are, and don't be silly. I'm sorry. It won't be very pleasant, but I've made up my mind to go, and I've got to tell him now.

THE MEMBER OF THE WEDDING

By Carson McCullers

Frankie Addams is a lonely, gangling overgrown twelve-year-old, an outsider, a member of no group. Berenice, the Negro housekeeper, is fond of Frankie, but does not always understand her.

Scene—*The kitchen of the Addams's house.*
Time—*August 1946.*

(Frankie *begins walking around the kitchen*)

Frankie. I expect Janice and Jarvis are almost to Winter Hill by now.

Berenice. Sit down. You make me nervous.

Frankie. Jarvis talked about Granny. He remembers her very good. But when I try to remember Granny, it is like her face is changing—like a face seen under water. Jarvis remembers Mother too, and I don't remember her at all.

Berenice. Naturally! Your mother died the day that you were born.

Frankie (*standing with one foot on the seat of the chair, leaning over the chair back, and laughing*) Did you hear what Jarvis said?

Berenice. What?

Frankie (*after laughing more*) They were talking about whether to vote for C. P. Macdonald. And Jarvis said, "Why I wouldn't vote for that scoundrel if he was running to be dog-catcher." I never heard anything so witty in my life.

(*A silence during which* Berenice *watches Frankie but does not speak*)

And you know what Janice remarked. When Jarvis mentioned about how much I've grown she said she didn't think I looked so terribly big. She said she got the major portion of her growth before she was thirteen. She said I was the right height and had acting talent and ought to go to Hollywood. She did, Berenice.

Berenice. O.K. All right. She did.

Frankie. She said she thought I was a lovely size and would probably not grow any taller. She said all fashion models and movie stars . . .

Berenice. She did not. I heard her from the window. She only remarked that you probably had already got your growth. But she didn't go on and on like that, or mention Hollywood.

63

FRANKIE. She said to me . . .

BERENICE. She said to you! This is a serious fault with you, Frankie. Somebody just makes a loose remark and you cozen it in your mind until nobody would recognize it. Your Aunt Pet happened to mention to Clorina that you had sweet manners and Clorina passed it on to you. For what it was worth. Then next thing I know you are going all around and bragging how Mrs West thought you had the finest manners in town and ought to go to Hollywood, and I don't know what all you didn't say. And that is a serious fault.

FRANKIE. Aw, quit preaching at me.

BERENICE. I ain't preaching. It's the solemn truth and you know it.

FRANKIE. I admit it a little. (*She sits at the table and puts her forehead on the palms of her hands. A pause, then she speaks softly*) What I need to know is this. Do you think I made a good impression?

BERENICE. Impression?

FRANKIE. Yes.

BERENICE. Well, how would I know?

FRANKIE. I mean, how did I act? What did I do?

BERENICE. Why, you didn't do anything to speak of.

FRANKIE. Nothing?

BERENICE. No. You just watched the pair of them like they was ghosts. Then, when they talked about the wedding, them ears of yours stiffened out, the size of cabbage leaves.

FRANKIE (*raising her hands to her ears*) They didn't.

BERENICE. They did.

FRANKIE. Some day you going to look down and find that big fat tongue of yours pulled out by the roots and laying there before you on the table.

BERENICE. Quit talking so rude.

FRANKIE (*after a pause*) I'm scared I didn't make a good impression.

BERENICE. What of it? I got a date with T.T. and he's supposed to pick me up here. I wish him and Honey would come on. You make me nervous.

(FRANKIE *sits miserably, her shoulders hunched. Then with a sudden gesture she bangs her forehead on the table. Her fists are clenched and she is sobbing*).

. . . Come on, don't act like that.

FRANKIE (*her voice muffled*) They were so pretty. They must have such a good time. And they went away and left me.

BERENICE. Sit up. Behave yourself.

FRANKIE. They came and went away, and left me with this feeling.

BERENICE. Hosee! I bet I know something. (*She begins tapping with her heel: one, two, three—bang! After a pause in which the rhythm is estab-*

lished she begins singing) Frankie's got a crush! Frankie's got a crush! Frankie's got a crush on the *wedding!*

FRANKIE. Quit!

BERENICE. Frankie's got a crush! Frankie's got a crush!

FRANKIE. You better quit! (*She rises suddenly and snatches up the carving knife*)

BERENICE. You lay down that knife.

FRANKIE. Make me. (*She bends the blade slowly*)

BERENICE. Lay it down, *Devil!* (*There is a silence*) Just throw it! You just!

(*After a pause Frankie aims the knife carefully at the closed door leading to the bedroom and throws it. The knife does not stick in the wall*)

FRANKIE. I used to be the best knife-thrower in this town.

BERENICE. Frances Addams, you goin' to try that stunt once too often.

FRANKIE. I warned you to quit pickin' with me.

BERENICE. You are not fit to live in a house.

FRANKIE. I won't be living in this one much longer: I'm going to run away from home.

BERENICE. And a good riddance to a big old bag of rubbish.

FRANKIE. You wait and see. I'm leavin' town.

BERENICE. And where do you think you are going?

FRANKIE (*gazing round the walls*) I don't know.

BERENICE. You're going crazy. That's where you goin'.

FRANKIE. No. (*Solemnly*) This coming Sunday after the wedding, I'm leaving town. And I swear to Jesus by my two eyes I'm never coming back here any more.

BERENICE (*going to Frankie and pushing her damp bangs from her forehead*) Sugar? You serious?

FRANKIE (*exasperated*) Of course! Do you think I would stand here and say that swear and tell a story? Sometimes, Bernice, I think it takes you longer to realize a fact than it does anybody who ever lived.

BERENICE. But you say you don't know where you going. You going but you don't know where. That don't make no sense to me.

FRANKIE (*after a long pause in which she again gazes around the walls of the room*) I feel just exactly like somebody has peeled all the skin off me. I wish I had some cold peach ice-cream.

(BERENICE *takes her by the shoulders*)

But every word I told you was the solemn truth. I'm leaving here after the wedding.

A MONTH IN THE COUNTRY

By Ivan Turgenev

Translated by Emlyn Williams

Natalia Petrovna, twenty-nine, the exquisitely beautiful, but discontented wife of a rich landowner, is enamoured by their son's new twenty-one-year-old tutor. Vera, Natalia's ward, is a beautiful, timid, immature and highly strung seventeen-year-old, who has also fallen in love with him. He returns no more than a respectful friendship and fondness for both.

Scene—*The drawing-room of Yslaev's house, on his estate in the country near Moscow.*

Time—*Early 1840's.*

Vera (*timidly*) Did you want me, Natalia Petrovna?
Natalia (*starting*) Ah, Verochka!
Vera. Do you feel quite well?
Natalia. Perfectly, it's a little close, that's all. Vera, I want to have a little talk with you.
Vera (*anxiously; putting down her music*) Oh? . . .
Natalia. A serious talk. Sit down, my dear, will you?

(Vera *sits*)

Now. . . . Vera, one thinks of you as still a child; but it's high time to give a thought to your future. You're an orphan, and not a rich one at that: sooner or later you are bound to tire of living on somebody else's property. Now how would you like suddenly to have control of your very own house?
Vera. I'm afraid I—I don't follow you, Natalia Petrovna . . .
Natalia. You are being sought in marriage.

(Vera *stares at her. A pause*)

You didn't expect this? I must confess I didn't either; you are still so young. I refuse to press you in the slightest—but I thought it my duty to let you know.

(*As* Vera *suddenly covers her face with her hands*)

Vera! My dear. . . . What is it? (*Taking her hands*) But you're shaking like a leaf!
Vera. Natalia Petrovna, I'm in your power. . . .
Natalia. In my power? Vera, what do you take me for? (*Cajoling*

66

as VERA *kisses her hands*) In my power, indeed—will you please take that back, this minute? I command you!

(*As* VERA *smiles through her tears*)

That's better. . . . (*Putting an arm round her, and drawing her nearer*) Vera, my child, I tell you what—you'll make believe I'm your elder sister—and we'll straighten out these strange things together—what do you say?

VERA. If you would like me to—yes . . .

NATALIA. Good. . . . Move closer—that's better. . . . First of all— as you're my sister, this is your home; so there's no possible question of anybody pining to be rid of you—now is that understood?

VERA (*whispering*) Yes. . . .

NATALIA. Now one fine day your sister comes to you and says, "What do you think, little one? Somebody is asking for your hand!" Well, what would be your first thought? That you're too young?

VERA. Just as you wish . . .

NATALIA. Now—now—does a girl say "just as you wish" to her sister?

VERA (*smiling*) Well, then, I'd just say, "I'm too young."

NATALIA. Good; your sister would agree, the suitor would be given "no" for an answer, fini. . . . But suppose he was a very nice gentleman with means, prepared to bide his time, in the hope that one day . . . what then?

VERA. Who is this suitor?

NATALIA. Ah, you're curious. Can't you guess?

VERA. No.

NATALIA. Bolshintsov.

VERA. Afanasy Ivanych?

NATALIA. Afanasy Ivanych. It's true he's not very young, and not wildly prepossessing . . .

(VERA *begins to laugh, then stops and looks at Natalia*)

VERA. You're joking. . . .

NATALIA (*after a pause, smiling*) No, but I see the matter is closed. If you had burst into tears when he was mentioned, there might have been some hope for him; but you laughed. . . . (*Rising, smiling wryly*) The matter is closed.

VERA. I'm sorry, but you took me completely by surprise. . . . Do people still get married at his age?

NATALIA. But how old do you take him for? He's on the right side of fifty!

VERA. I suppose he is, but he has *such* a peculiar face. . . .

NATALIA. Bolshintsov, my dear, you are dead and buried, may you rest in peace. . . . It was foolish of me to forget that little girls dream of marrying for love.

VERA. But, Natalia Petrovna . . . didn't *you* marry for love?

NATALIA (*after a pause*) Yes, of course I did. . . . Eh, bien, fini!

Bolshintsov, you are dismissed. . . . I must confess I never much fancied that puffy old moon-face next to your fresh young cheek. There! . . . (*Sitting again, next to Vera*) And you're not frightened of me any more?

VERA. No, not any more. . . .

NATALIA. Well, then, Verochka darling, just whisper quietly in my ear . . . you don't want to marry Bolshintsov because he's too old and far from an Adonis—but is that the only reason?

VERA (*after a pause*) Natalia Petrovna, isn't it reason enough?

NATALIA. Undoubtedly, my dear . . . but you haven't answered my question.

(*Pause*)

VERA. There's no other reason.

NATALIA. Oh. . . . Of course, that puts the matter on rather a different footing.

VERA. How do you mean, Natalia Petrovna?

NATALIA. I realize you can never fall in *love* with Bolshintsov; but he's an excellent man. And if there is nobody else. . . . Isn't there *anybody* you're fond of?

VERA. Well, there's you, and little Kolia . . .

NATALIA (*with a hint of impatience*) Vera, you must know what I mean. . . . Out of the young men you've met . . . have you formed any attachment at all?

VERA. I quite like one or two, but . . .

NATALIA. For instance, don't I remember at the Krinitsins your dancing three times with a tall officer—what was his name . . . ?

VERA. With a long moustache? (*Smiling*) He giggled all the time.

NATALIA. Oh. . . . (*After a pause*) What about our philosopher Rakitin?

VERA. Mihail Alexandrovich? I'm very fond of him, of course, who wouldn't be. . . .

NATALIA. An elder brother, I see. . . . (*Suddenly*) And the new tutor?

(*Pause*)

VERA. Alexei Nikolaich?

NATALIA. Alexei Nikolaich.

VERA. I like him very much. (*She has blushed*)

(NATALIA *is watching her narrowly*)

NATALIA. He *is* nice, isn't he? Such a pity he's so bashful with everybody. . . .

VERA (*innocently*) Oh, he isn't bashful with me!

NATALIA. Isn't he?

VERA. I suppose it's because we're both orphans. I think he must appear shy to you because he's afraid of you. You see, he's had no chance to know you. . . .

NATALIA. Afraid of me? How do you know?

VERA. He told me so.

NATALIA. He told you. . . .

VERA. Don't you like him, Natalia Petrovna?

NATALIA. He seems very kind-hearted.

VERA. Oh, he is! If you only knew. . . . (*Turning to her enthusiastically*) The whole of this household loves him—he's so warm, once he's got over his shyness—the other day an old beggar-woman had to be taken to hospital—do you know he carried her the whole way? And one day he picked a flower for me off a cliff—he's as nimble as a reindeer. D'you remember yesterday, when he cleared that tremendous ditch? And he's always so good-tempered and gay. . . .

NATALIA. That doesn't sound a bit like him—when he's with me, he . . .

VERA. But that's what I mean, Natalia Petrovna, it's because he doesn't know you! I'll tell him how truly kind you are. . . .

NATALIA (*rising; ironically*) Thank you, my dear. . . .

VERA. You'll soon see the difference—because he listens to what I say, though I *am* younger than he is . . .

NATALIA. I never knew you two were such friends. You must be careful, Vera.

VERA. Careful?

NATALIA. I know he's a very pleasant young man, but at your age, it's not quite . . . People might think. . . .

(VERA *blushes, and looks down*)

Don't be impatient, my dear, will you, if I seem to be laying down the law? We older people regard it as our business to plague the young with our "don'ts" and "mustn'ts". But, as you like him, and nothing more, there's no real need for me to say another word. (*Sitting next to her again*) Is there?

VERA (*raising her eyes, timidly*) He . . .

NATALIA. Vera, is that the way to look at a sister? (*Caressing her*) If your *real* sister asked you very quietly, "Verochka, what exactly are your feelings towards So-and-so?" . . . What would you answer?

(*As* VERA *looks at her, hesitating*)

Those eyes are dying to tell me something. . . .

(VERA *suddenly presses her head to Natalia's breast.* NATALIA *bites her lips*)

My poor Vera. . . .

VERA (*without raising her head*) Oh dear. . . . I don't know what's the matter with me. . . .

NATALIA. My poor sweet . . .

(*As* VERA *presses herself closer to her*)

And he . . . what of him?

VERA. I don't know. . . .

NATALIA. Vera, what of him?

VERA. I don't know, I tell you. . . . Sometimes I imagine . . .

NATALIA. You imagine what?

VERA (*her face hidden*) That I see a look in his eyes . . . as if he thought of me—as a special person—perhaps. . . . (*Disengages herself, trying to be calm*) Oh, I don't know. (*She raises her head, and sees the expression on Natalia's face*) What's the matter, Natalia Petrovna?

(NATALIA *is staring at her, as if she were a stranger*)

NATALIA. The matter? . . . (*Recovering*) What did you say? Nothing . . .

VERA. But there *is* something the matter! (*Rising*) I'll ring . . .

NATALIA. No, no—don't ring . . . (*louder*) please! It's passed off already. You go back to your music—and we—we'll talk another time.

VERA. You're not angry with me, Natalia Petrovna?

NATALIA. Not in the least. . . . I just want to be by myself.

(VERA *tries to take her hand;* NATALIA *turns away as if she had not noticed her gesture*)

VERA (*tears in her eyes*) Natalia Petrovna. . . .

NATALIA. Please. . . .

(VERA *goes slowly back to the ballroom.* NATALIA *does not move*)

These children love each other. . . . Well, it's a touching idea, and may Heaven bless them both. The way she came out with it . . . and I with no idea—(*laughing feverishly*) ha! (*Rising, vehement*) But all is not lost—oh, no. . . . (*Stopping and collecting herself*) But I don't know myself any more—what am I doing? (*After a pause, deliberately*) Shall I tell you, Natalia Petrovna? You're trying to marry a poor orphan girl to a foolish old man—you've gone as far as to use that wily old doctor as a go-between. . . . Then there's your philosopher, and then your husband . . . what is happening—(*panic-stricken, her hands to her face*) what is happening? (*After a pause, slowly*) Unhappy woman, for the first time in your life . . . you are in love.

VERA *begins to play on the piano;* NATALIA *listens, and walks slowly and dreamily out into the garden.*

NATIONAL VELVET

By Enid Bagnold

A strange affinity exists between Mrs Brown, an ex-Channel swimmer, and her fourteen-year-old daughter, Velvet. Velvet's love for horses is fostered by Mi, Mr Brown's odd-job man, and he has the ability to inspire her, in the way his father inspired Mrs Brown in training her for her Channel swim.

VELVET *is inside the house, looking out of the window.* MRS BROWN *is outside, by the window.*

VELVET. Mi gone?
MRS BROWN (*without looking round*) He's gone.
VELVET. Kin I come out?
MRS BROWN. You kin please yourself. . . .

(VELVET *comes over the window-sill and sits by her mother's chair, facing front.* MRS BROWN *does not move*)

VELVET. Mother . . . (*Pause, no answer*) I bin thinkin' of Edwina. (*No answer. She looks up at her mother*) S'awful to grow up.
MRS BROWN. Nope.
VELVET. Why isn't it?
MRS BROWN. Things come suitable to the time. (*Pause*) Lot o' nonsense talked about growin' up. (*Pause*) Childbirth. An' bein' in love. An' death. You can't know 'em till you come to them. No use guessin' an' dreading. You kin call it pain. But what's pain? Depends on how you are an' how you take it. (*Pause*) Don't you dread nothin', Velvet.
VELVET. But you're so mighty, like a tree.
MRS BROWN. There's one thing, Velvet.
VELVET. What's that?
MRS BROWN. Pray to God you don't get fat.
VELVET (*throws her arms round the beloved great knees and kisses them, looking up into her mother's face*) Mother, Mother, . . . you get us all beat. Mi thinks you're Godalmighty. 'N' we all do.
MRS BROWN (*looking down at last at the child*) Chut, child. Don't mount up in a torment. 'M' not grumbling. What came on me, came on me an' I don't change nothin' underneath.
VELVET. All the same 'sawful to grow up. All this getting ready and getting ready for something. I don't ever want children. Only horses.
MRS BROWN (*steadily*) Who can tell?

VELVET. I've got me. (*Putting her hand on her chest*) I can't ever be anything else but me.

MRS BROWN (*offhand*) You're all safe. You got both of us, you an' me. Say your prayers now an' get along.

VELVET. Not yet; not yet;

MRS BROWN. Say your prayers, I say. Plunging off this time o' night an' getting your mind all in a daze an' a worry! Say 'em, I say.

VELVET (*kneeling*) Ah . . . v'Farver . . . eh . . . art'n'eav'n . . . mn . . . mn . . . mn . . . poweranaglory . . . amen . . . Mother!

MRS BROWN. Nice sort a mumble. Yes?

VELVET. You're all right, aren't you?

MRS BROWN. I'm as good as living for ever.

VELVET. Do you know what I say when I say real prayers?

MRS BROWN. Isn't the Lord's Prayer good enough?

VELVET. I say . . . (*Kneeling up, in earnest, putting her hands together, and staring wide-eyed at her mother*) "God" I say . . . I say . . . "God! Give me horses. . . . Oh, God, give me horses! Let me be . . . let me be . . . the best rider in England." (*She speaks this wonderfully, without sentiment, never taking her eyes off her mother, who looks back at her*) Mi said he'd make a miracle.

MRS BROWN. What's that?

VELVET. He said I was to keep my faith and that a miracle would happen.

NO ROOM AT THE INN

By Joan Temple

When Mary O'Rane's mother dies, the twelve-year-old girl is billeted in the overcrowded house of the slatternly Mrs. Voray. Her kind young teacher, Judith Drave, tries to help her.

SCENE—*Mrs Voray's house.*
TIME—*During the last war.*

JUDITH. Mary dear . . .

MARY (*swallowing with difficulty*) Yes, Mrs Drave?

JUDITH. I—I don't really know what to say to you, chicken. It isn't too nice here, is it?

MARY. I—I think it's dreadful!

JUDITH. Well—well, perhaps not quite so bad as that. But it's not what you've been used to. Look here! Try and stick it out for a day or two, will you? Meantime I'll ask all round—get into touch with some of the mothers and see if one of them will take you in. Daddy's away at sea, isn't he?

MARY. Yes, Mrs Drave.

JUDITH. Know when he'll be back?

MARY. No, No, I don't.

JUDITH. But he might come back any day, mightn't he?

MARY. Yes!

JUDITH. That's something to look forward to, isn't it?

MARY. Yes.

JUDITH. Well, then, I'll be trying everywhere to find a nice home for you, and there's the chance of your father coming home—why, perhaps tomorrow or the day after!—so stick it here for a bit, will you? Do your best to stick it for a bit.

MARY. I—I'll try, Mrs Drave. But—I do miss my mummy so!

JUDITH. You *must* do, poor child!

MARY. She's been dead such a long time. (*She stretches out her hand and looks at her wrist-watch, which is much too loose for her*) Twenty-nine hours and three-quarters!

JUDITH. That's Mummy's watch?

MARY. Yes.

JUDITH. The strap's a bit loose. Let me alter it for you.

(MARY *takes off her wrist-watch and* JUDITH *adjusts the strap*)

You must take great care of this. And keep it always.

MARY. Oh, *yes*, Mrs Drave!

JUDITH (*handing back the watch*) There you are, my dear.

(MARY *puts the watch on again*)

I think you're splendid, not to cry.

MARY. I cried so much yesterday, I don't think I've got any water left in me.

JUDITH. Well, try not to cry any more, darling. Things are never as bad as they seem.

MARY (*surprised*) But Mummy's dead!

JUDITH. Oh, Mary, I didn't mean that! What a stupid thing for me to say! What I really meant was—you not having a home. Something will turn up, I feel sure. Feel like coming to school tomorrow?

MARY. I—I don't know.

JUDITH. It might help.

MARY. But when I come out of school I—I'd have to come back here!

JUDITH. Only for a little while. But in school—you and I will have a secret. *You*'ll be saying to *me*: "I'm sticking it out! I'm being brave!" And *I*'ll be saying to *you*: "I *know* you're being brave, Mary!" So try and come, will you?

MARY. Yes, I'll try.

JUDITH. That's the ticket. Well, I must be getting along. (*She stoops quickly and kisses Mary*) Good night, Mary.

MARY. Good night, Mrs Drave.

JUDITH, *with a worried backward look at Mary, goes out, closing the door.*

ONE WAY PENDULUM

By N. F. Simpson

Mabel Groomkirby, forty-five, brisk, busy and preoccupied with household activities frequently procures the services of a "professional eater of left-over food", the enormously fat Myra Gantry.

Scene—*The Groomkirby's sitting-room.*
Period—*Modern.*

MABEL. It's the same with his parking meters.

MYRA. Like Mr Gantry with his.

MABEL. Five of them altogether he's got out there, in different places. Round the lawn and up by the rockery. But once he's put his sixpence in there's no budging him. He'll stand there like a statue till his hour's up.

MYRA. Mr Gantry generally takes a book out there with him.

MABEL. Instead of going away after he's stood there for ten minutes or so and having sixpenn'orth in front of one of the others. What's the good of *having* five? And the consequence is, of course, that when he goes round to empty them all at the end of the month he's got practically nothing to show for hours of waiting. And he's out in all weathers.

MYRA. It's the only way they can save anything.

MABEL. He's afraid of anything that's got the least suggestion of overcharging about it. Unless he gets his full hour once he's put his sixpence in, he feels he's been done in some way. He's frightened he'll end up losing his own custom.

MYRA. If you don't speculate you don't accumulate.

MABEL. I tell him, by the time it came to losing his own custom—if it ever did—he could have made enough overcharging himself to pay somebody to stand in front of them twenty-four hours a day. And make his fortune practically. But he can't seem to see it.

MYRA (*scooping potatoes and carrots on to her plate*) They don't, Mabel. Once they get an idea in their heads. (*She pauses*) You've still got your Aunt Mildred, I see.

MABEL. She's in the Outer Hebrides. Waiting for a train back to St Pancras.

MYRA (*after a pause*) She lives for her transport, doesn't she?

MABEL. We're trying to get a tricycle for her—but they don't seem to make them side-saddle any more.

(*There is a long pause.* MYRA *scoops meat on to her plate*)

MYRA. You heard about Mr Gridlake?

MABEL. No?

MYRA. I thought you might have heard. Had an accident on his skis.

MABEL. Serious?

MYRA. Killed himself.

MABEL. No!

MYRA. It was his own fault. He went down the incline, round the bend and straight into the jaws of death.

MABEL (*after a pause*) What on earth for?

MYRA. Showing off, I suppose.

MABEL (*after a pause*) You'd think he'd have had more sense.

MYRA (*after a pause*) He hadn't intended staying there, of course.

MABEL (*after a pause*) In one side and out the other, I suppose.

MYRA. With his skis on sideways.

MABEL. Sideways?

MYRA (*after a pause*) Thought he could nip in one side and out the other before death could tell which way he was going. Trying to take death in by putting his skis on the wrong way round. (*She pauses*) I feel sorry for Mrs Gridlake.

MABEL. What actually happened in there? Missed his footing, I suppose?

MYRA. I'll tell you what *I* think happened, Mabel.

MABEL. Too confident.

MYRA. No. What I think happened was that he went in all right, and then caught his head a glancing blow as he was coming out. (*She pauses*) It's easily done. Especially a tall man.

MABEL. Stunned himself.

MYRA. Stunned himself, and then of course it was too late.

MABEL (*after a pause*) Instead of *allowing* for his height.

MYRA. Allow for it? I don't suppose he even knew what it was.

MABEL (*in remonstrance*) Oh! But he must have done! I can't believe he didn't know his own height, Myra.

MYRA. Mr Gantry doesn't.

MABEL. Do you mean to say he doesn't know how tall he is?

MYRA. He's not all that certain how short he is, Mabel, if it comes to that.

MABEL. It's about time you made him have himself measured, Myra.

MYRA. The same with his weight. He has to work it out every time.

(MRS GROOMKIRBY *maintains a silence of disapprobation*)

MYRA (*after a pause*) I didn't tell you about the summer before last, did I? When he went over the edge at Scarborough?

MABEL. No?

MYRA. Yes—he fell off one of the cliffs playing dominoes with the children.

MABEL. I never knew that.

MYRA. How long do you think it took him to get to the bottom?

(MRS GROOMKIRBY *looks inquiringly*)

MYRA. Three hours!

MABEL. No!

MYRA. All but five minutes.

MABEL. But what was he *doing?*

MYRA. Working out his weight, if you please.

MABEL. Not on the way down!

MYRA. On the way down, Mabel. He'd left his diary, with his weight and everything in it, back at the caravan.

MABEL. Wouldn't it have done when he got home?

MYRA. It was a question of knowing how hard to fall, Mabel. He needed to know his weight before he could work it out. (*She pauses*) And then after all that, he found he'd fallen harder than he need have done. Made a mistake with one of the figures or something.

MABEL. It's easily done.

MYRA (*after a pause*) Any other man would have known his weight, of course.

MABEL. You should make him carry his diary about with him, Myra.

THE ORCHARD WALLS

By R. F. DELDERFIELD

Shirley Grant, a seventeen-year-old schoolgirl has attempted suicide because she is to be separated from her boy friend. Her sympathetic headmistress, Chris Muir, is able to offer Shirley understanding and wisdom.

SCENE—*The Principal's study at Mellingham Collegiate School for Girls.*
PERIOD—*Modern.*

CHRIS. Rachel's making you some tea. (*She sees the newspaper on the desk, picks it up and puts it in the drawer*) Where is your mother now, Shirley? (*Firmly*) Your mother! Where is she?
SHIRLEY (*slowly collecting herself*) She's at home, Miss Muir.
CHRIS. I shall have to tell her you're here. She'll be looking for you.
SHIRLEY (*rising suddenly*) I'll go now.
CHRIS (*sharply*) Sit down and stay where you are!

(SHIRLEY *sits.* CHRIS *glances at her watch*)

What's your home number?
SHIRLEY. You needn't—ring. I said I was going to Ginnersley's, the leather shop. Mother was meeting me there. I had—to buy labels and an attache-case.
CHRIS. What time was she meeting you?
SHIRLEY. At four-thirty, Miss Muir. I gave my word of honour I wouldn't try and see Mike.
CHRIS. *Have* you seen him?
SHIRLEY. No. I tried to but he wasn't there.
CHRIS. It's gone three-thirty now. When are you leaving Mellingham?
SHIRLEY. Tomorrow.
CHRIS. By yourself?
SHIRLEY. Mother's coming to London, we're going to stay there until Friday.
CHRIS (*crossing to the armchair*) Do you think it's at all possible that your mother could go with you to Canada?
SHIRLEY (*sullenly*) I don't want her to, I'd sooner anything than she did.
CHRIS. Somebody will have to. You can't be trusted to go by yourself after this, can you?

(SHIRLEY *is silent, hunched and miserable. Suddenly* CHRIS *succumbs*

78

to impulse. She sits on the upper arm and lets her hand pass over Shirley's hair)

Don't you think—can't you see that what you were going to do would have been a terribly cruel thing to do to Michael? Is that love, deliberately hurting anyone as much as that?

(Her words and manner have the effect of relaxing SHIRLEY. *She suddenly turns towards her and begins to sob.* CHRIS *takes her in her arms and strokes her hair. The buzzer goes.* CHRIS *gently disengages herself and gets up.*

CHRIS *goes out* L. *She is absent a few seconds.* SHIRLEY *recovers, blows her nose.*

CHRIS *returns with a cup of tea)*

Better now?

*(*SHIRLEY *nods and gives another hard blow)*

Here, drink this. *(She passes the tea)*

SHIRLEY *(suddenly)* Couldn't you see mother again? Couldn't you explain? I wouldn't care if I didn't see him, if I just knew he was there, when I passed the garage . . .

CHRIS. You've got to make that trip, Shirley. You've got to make it in spite of everything and I think you're going to do it. If I thought you wouldn't I'd have to tell your mother and the police straight away. Drink your tea.

*(*SHIRLEY *drinks. She sets down the cup)*

Now listen to me. Who will you be going to in Vancouver?

SHIRLEY. Mother's sister. She's married to a doctor there.

CHRIS. I don't suppose it'll be half as bad as you imagine—oh, I know you'll mope a bit at first, but there'll be compensations, a new country, new experiences, even new friends if you don't shut them out.

SHIRLEY. You've been terribly kind. But even you don't really understand.

CHRIS *(crossing below the armchair to* C) Listen, Shirley, listen to me carefully. I've understood all along, but whether the people around us are hostile or whether they're friendly and helpful, all the big things in life have to be faced alone and all the really important decisions made without help or advice. You imagine now that if you were allowed to stay with Michael he could decide everything concerning your joint future but he couldn't, no matter how much he loves you or you him, and it wouldn't be right if he could. Love isn't a mere surrender of responsibilities on the woman's part, Shirley, it's much, much more of a share-out. When you wrote that letter, and went up into the tower just now, you weren't being heroic and romantic, you were just leaving Michael to face the consequences of what you did, and face them quite alone.

SHIRLEY (*rising*) He would have understood, I know he would have understood the moment he got my note.

CHRIS (*moving behind the armcnair*) Your *note*. (*She speaks almost contemptuously*) "I have a rendezvous with death at some disputed barricade . . ." Do you imagine Alan Seeger wrote that in a mood of weakness and surrender?

SHIRLEY. He wasn't afraid to die.

CHRIS. Good heavens, child, of course he wasn't, but he didn't throw away his life because he ran into a personal problem that hurt. That poem isn't an excuse, it's a challenge! There's something else you've forgotten too. Suppose you'd succeeded in—in what you thought about doing. Do you imagine you would have lived on in Michael's memory as something sweet and wonderful, that happened to him when he was young? Wouldn't you have stayed there as something horrible and frightening, so that all his life he'd have tried and tried to forget you?

SHIRLEY (*breaking down* L) No, that isn't true!

CHRIS (*crossing to* L *of Shirley*) It *is* true, Shirley, terribly true, and if he'd been lucky he might have been able to do it—with some other girl, someone who showed him gentleness and tenderness and a love that was really worth something; (*deliberately*) somebody who was able to convince him that he wasn't halfway to being a murderer.

SHIRLEY. No!

(SHIRLEY *rushes out up* C, *leaving the door open.* CHRIS *leans dejectedly against the mantelpiece.*

After a pause, SHIRLEY *returns slowly and stands in the doorway*)

If he'd have been at the garage, if I could have seen him once more, for a few minutes.

CHRIS (*turning*) You *are* going to see him, Shirley. I sent for him. His father's letting him come over. You'll only have a few minutes together.

SHIRLEY (*much calmer*) If that's true I'll be all right. I swear I'll be all right, Miss Muir!

CHRIS (*gently*) I know you will, Shirley.

(CHRIS *tears up Shirley's note and drops it in the waste-paper basket as she crosses to sit at her desk. The choir is heard singing "Greensleeves"*)

There's the choir practice; Miss Raynor's determined we win the County Cup again.

SHIRLEY (*closing the door*) It's funny, I haven't remembered the days since I left here last week.

CHRIS. Does it seem all that time ago?

SHIRLEY. Like looking back to when you were a child.

CHRIS. Will you go to school again in Canada?

SHIRLEY. I hope not.

CHRIS. You haven't been unhappy here until this week, have you?

SHIRLEY. Until you came I was.

CHRIS (*smiling*) It's nice of you to say that, but I don't think it's quite true, Shirley.

SHIRLEY. Yes it is, Miss Muir. (*She crosses to the desk*)

CHRIS. When you're in Canada—have you made any sort of arrangement to write to Michael?

SHIRLEY. I won't be allowed to, not for two years.

CHRIS. Did you agree to that?

SHIRLEY. I had to. Mother said if I did write, or he wrote to me, she'd find a way to get him into serious trouble.

CHRIS. I see. (*Pause*) Would you care to write—to me?

SHIRLEY. Yes I would, Miss Muir.

CHRIS. Very well. Promise you'll write whenever you feel like it.

(SHIRLEY *comes* C *as the choir fades*)

SHIRLEY. Miss Muir.

CHRIS. Yes?

SHIRLEY (*moving* C) Mike won't have to—he won't have to know about what happened, will he?

CHRIS. From now on that's rather up to you, Shirley.

SHIRLEY (*moving above the armchair*) But besides you there's Rachel, and Miss Maynard and Mr Barber, the organist.

CHRIS. I'll speak to them all, after you've gone.

(*The buzzer goes*)

RACHEL (*off; on the intercom*) He's here now, Miss Muir.

CHRIS (*on the intercom*) All right, Rachel, thank you. (*She picks up the exercise books and crosses to the door. To Shirley*) Michael's here now. It's a quarter past four. You've got less than ten minutes. You won't let me down again, will you?

SHIRLEY. No, I promise. Miss Muir?

CHRIS. Yes?

SHIRLEY. Could you—would you lend me your compact?

(CHRIS *smiles, returns and takes her handbag from the desk*)

CHRIS. Here. (*She gives Shirley her powder compact and mirror*) Don't overdo it.

A PHOENIX TOO FREQUENT

By Christopher Fry

Dynamene is a beautiful Ephesian widow, who, with her devoted maid, Doto, has determined to die upon her husband's tomb. She is interrupted by a young soldier, whose chatter she finds most attractive, and she is torn between dying for her husband and living for this new love.

Scene—*The tomb of Virilius, near Ephesus; night.*

DYNAMENE.	Hurry, hurry!
DOTO.	Yes, Madam, hurry; of course. Are we there Already? How nice. Death doesn't take Any doing at all. We were gulped into Hades As easy as an oyster.
DYNAMENE.	Doto! Hurry, hurry,
DOTO.	Yes, madam.—But they've taken out all my bones. I haven't a bone left. I'm a Shadow: wonderfully shady In the legs. We shall have to sit out eternity, madam, If they've done the same to you.
DYNAMENE.	You'd better wake up. If you can't go to sleep again, you'd better wake up. Oh dear.—We're still alive, Doto, do you hear me?
DOTO.	You must speak for yourself, madam. I'm quite dead. I'll tell you how I know. I feel Invisible. I'm a wraith, madam; I'm only Waiting to be wafted.
DYNAMENE.	If only you *would* be. Do you see where you are? Look. Do you see?
DOTO.	Yes. You're right, madam. We're still alive. Isn't it enough to make you swear? Here we are, dying to be dead, And where does it get us?
DYNAMENE.	Perhaps you should try to die. In some other place. Yes! Perhaps the air here Suits you too well. You were sleeping very heavily.
DOTO.	And all the time you alone and dying. I shouldn't have. Has the corporal been long gone, Madam?
DYNAMENE.	He came and went, came and went, You know the way.
DOTO.	Very well I do. And went

82

He should have, come he should never. Oh dear, he must
Have disturbed you, madam.

DYNAMENE.   He could be said
To've disturbed me. Listen; I have something to say
to you.

DOTO.   I expect so, madam. Maybe I *could* have kept him out
But men are in before I wish they wasn't.
I think quickly enough, but I get behindhand
With what I ought to be saying. It's a kind of stammer
In my way of life, madam.

DYNAMENE.   I have been unkind,
I have sinfully wronged you, Doto.

DOTO.   Never, madam.

DYNAMENE. Oh yes. I was letting you die with me, Doto, without
Any fair reason. I was drowning you
In grief that wasn't yours. That was wrong, Doto.

DOTO.   But I haven't got anything against dying, madam.
I may *like* the situation, as far as I like
Any situation, madam. Now if you'd said mangling,
A lot of mangling, I might have thought twice about
staying.
We all have our dislikes, madam.

DYNAMENE.   I'm asking you
To leave me, Doto, at once, as quickly as possible,
Now, before—now, Doto, and let me forget
My bad mind which confidently expected you
To companion me to Hades. Now goodbye,
Goodbye.

DOTO.   No, it's not goodbye at all.
I shouldn't know another night of sleep, wondering
How you got on, or what I was missing, come to that.
I should be anxious about you too. When you belong
To an upper class, the netherworld might come
strange.
Now I was born nether, madam, though not
As nether as some. No, it's not goodbye, madam.

DYNAMENE. Oh, Doto, go; you must, you must! And if I seem
Without gratitude, forgive me. It isn't so,
It is far, far from so. But I can only
Regain my peace of mind if I know you're gone.

DOTO.   Besides, look at the time, madam. Where should I go
At three in the morning? Even if I was to think
Of going; and think of it I never shall.

DYNAMENE. Think of the unmatchable world, Doto.

DOTO.   I do
Think of it, madam. And when I think of it, what
Have I thought? Well, it depends, madam.

DYNAMENE.　　　　　　　　　　　　　　　　　I insist,
　　　Obey me. At once. Doto.
DOTO.　　　　　　　　　　　　　　　　　Here I sit.
DYNAMENE. What shall I do with you?
DOTO.　　　　　　　　　　　　Ignore me, madam.
　　　I know my place. I shall die quite unobtrusive.
　　　Oh, look, the corporal's forgotten to take his equip-
　　　　　ment.
DYNAMENE. Could he be so careless?
DOTO.　　　　　　　　　I shouldn't hardly have thought so.
　　　Poor fellow. They'll go and deduct it off his credits.
　　　I suppose, madam, I suppose he couldn't be thinking
　　　Of coming back?
DYNAMENE. He'll think of these. He will notice
　　　He isn't wearing them. He'll come; he is sure to come.
DOTO.　　　Oh.
DYNAMENE.　　　I know he will.
DOTO.　　　　　　　　　　Oh, oh.
　　　Is that all for tonight, madam? May I go now,
　　　　madam?
DYNAMENE. Doto. Will　you?
DOTO.　　　　　　　　　Just you try to stop me, madam.
　　　Sometimes going is a kind of instinct with me.
　　　I'll leave death to some other occasion.
DYNAMENE.　　　　　　　　　　　　　Do,
　　　Doto. Any other time. Now you must hurry.
　　　I won't delay you from life another moment.
　　　Oh, Doto, good-bye.
DOTO.　　　　　　　　　Good-bye. Life is unusual,
　　　Isn't it, madam? Remember me to Cerberus.

THE PLAYER QUEEN

By KATHLEEN STAFFORD

Queen Elizabeth I has discovered that a young lady-in-waiting, Katherine, has left the court to appear in William Shakespeare's play "Romeo and Juliet".

SCENE—*An ante-room in Whitehall Palace.*
TIME—*June 1602.*

ELIZABETH. How came you by these words?
KATHERINE. They were given me, Your Majesty.
ELIZABETH. By whom?
KATHERINE. By a poet, madam.
ELIZABETH. What is his name?

(KATHERINE *does not answer*)

What is his name?
KATHERINE. Mr Shakespeare, Your Majesty.
ELIZABETH. Mr Shakespeare, the playwright.
KATHERINE. Yes, Your Majesty.
ELIZABETH. These words are from a play—are they not.
KATHERINE (*very quietly*) Yes, madam.
ELIZABETH. How came Mr Shakespeare to give them to you?
KATHERINE. I love poetry, madam.
ELIZABETH. So you love poetry. That doesn't answer my question. May I ask how you became so familiar with these words—or perhaps you are familiar with the poet? That is more likely.

(KATHERINE *does not answer*)

Answer me, girl. (*Furiously*) I say perhaps you are familiar with the poet?
KATHERINE (*vehemently*) *No*—Your Majesty.
ELIZABETH. So you have time apparently to learn poetry but not enough time to attend to your duties. Where were you this evening? They told me you were ill in bed—that I do not believe, so don't waste time telling me lies.

(KATHERINE *again hesitates*)

Where were you?
KATHERINE. I was out, Your Majesty. (*She hesitates*) I went to a play.
ELIZABETH. You went to a play? Alone?

85

KATHERINE. Yes, madam. (*With lowered eyes*) I went to Mr Shakespeare's play—*Romeo and Juliet*. (*She raises her eyes timorously*) At my Lord Greville's house.

ELIZABETH (*watching her closely*) Was that all you did?

KATHERINE (*in a low voice*) No, Your Majesty.

ELIZABETH. What else did you do? Answer me, girl.

KATHERINE (*slowly stating a truth*) I—*acted* in the play, Your Majesty.

ELIZABETH. You—acted—in—the—play? Do I hear aright? One of my ladies became a common player? Is this true, or have you taken leave of your senses?

KATHERINE. It is true, madam.

ELIZABETH (*furiously*) You must be mad. (*She strikes her*) How dare you behave in this disgusting and unspeakable manner. A woman acting in a play, that is bad enough, but that it should be one of my ladies-in-waiting. You are shameless. You imagine you're in love with this playwright, I suppose, therefore he can persuade you to forget yourself and your duty so far as to reduce you to the level of a drab—a trollop. This Mr Shakespeare shall be taught a lesson he will not forget. Do not dare answer me. I will teach you also that you cannot lightly hold the service of the Queen up to ridicule—you shall be soundly whipped, and kept under lock and key. (*Contemptuously*) This emotion you are pleased to call love reduces women to the level of animals.

KATHERINE (*throwing herself on to her knees*) Your Majesty—you are unjust. I am not in love with Mr Shakespeare—I am not in love with anyone—unless . . .

ELIZABETH. Unless?

KATHERINE. Unless I'm in love with acting. (*Passionately*) Oh, Your Majesty—please listen—I want to be a player. Why should it be left to boys to take women's parts?

ELIZABETH. You are out of your mind, girl! It's unheard of—it could never be. A woman player—you don't know what you say.

KATHERINE (*desperately*) Look at us here. Look at our useless lives. Madam, believe me—I'm not in love or ever have been, but to-night I was happy because I did the thing I longed to do. One day, Your Majesty, women will act in plays and no-one will think it wrong or unusual.

ELIZABETH (*after a pause*) There may be some truth in this, but how can you at twenty know what is best for women? They've always been the home-makers. Why should they suddenly want to change? Because you have this mad desire you imagine all women must be the same. First and foremost they will desire lovers—a home —children. These emotions will predominate and influence their actions now and always.

(KATHERINE *is silent*)

Well, girl? Is not that so?

KATHERINE (*quietly*) No, Your Majesty, ~~not altogether.~~

ELIZABETH. ~~Come!~~ You are obstinate. You talked just now of the unhappiness of my ladies. Perhaps you can tell me why their lives here are made so ~~unbearably~~ miserable. I am waiting.

KATHERINE (*with difficulty*) You are a great Queen, madam. What should you know of our lives? ~~We mustn't show our~~ feelings. Whether we are happy or unhappy is no matter to *you* . . . (*She checks herself*)

ELIZABETH. Well?

KATHERINE. Madam, I can't explain—you are so different from us. All your life has been as you have *made* it—~~as you have *wanted* it.~~ *We* are given no choice. We live at home or here—it doesn't matter where—and wait for husbands. ~~We must attract and please—that is all.~~ (*She stops again*) Your Majesty, I've said too much already—please let me go.

ELIZABETH. I command you to finish.

KATHERINE. Some women do not wish for more. ~~Dorothy is one of those. She is gay and lighthearted. So long as she can dance and have lovers, she is happy. Ann only wants to marry and live quietly with the man she loves, but Phillipa would like to be a scholar. Women cannot do these things and so~~ her energies are wasted on anxiety for her brother. She is bored and unhappy—~~ill-tempered often because her life has so little meaning.~~ (*She stops*) Forgive me, madam . . . I have talked too much—*please* let me go!

(*There is a long pause.* ELIZABETH *moves down below the chair* LC *and then turns to Katherine*)

ELIZABETH. So my life has been happy and as I wanted it. ~~You think I've lived doing always the things I liked.~~

KATHERINE. Perhaps not all the time, but you've gifts, madam, which you've been able to use. You lead men and women—you've made England a great country. You didn't want a husband and children because . . .

ELIZABETH. *Enough!* (*She pauses, then sits in the chair* LC) How do you or anyone else know what I wanted or did not want?

KATHERINE (*frightened at Elizabeth's vehemence*) Your Majesty, ~~I'm sorry—I——~~

ELIZABETH. ~~Come nearer—listen to me.~~

(KATHERINE *takes a pace towards Elizabeth and stands waiting. The* QUEEN *continues, slowly and deliberately. There is no attempt at pathos or self-pity. For a few moments she reveals to Katherine the feelings and desires of her youth—the fact that she too may have wanted to follow some other course*)

At twenty-five years of age I became Queen. Was I asked whether that was what I wanted to do? ~~Whether that was the life I should choose?~~ Was I asked whether I should be *happy* as you call it? My feelings were not even considered. England needed a Queen ~~and I was next in succession—not an enviable position at that time—or at any time. I was twenty-five, remember, and~~ it never occurred to anyone that I might have wanted to marry and have children. ~~It was never suggested that I might have other desires.~~ Remember also that I wasn't nurtured wholly with the thought that I should one day be a Queen—my life had been uncertain—precarious. Not many years before my accession I was thrust into the Tower. On the day of my Coronation, when I heard the cheers of the people, I knew how fickle and changeable those same people could be. How easily the blessings might turn to curses. I also knew there was no escape for me—that in future my feelings as a woman would not count—my personal desires mattered not at all. The country was in a state of chaos, without direction and needed a ruler. I was a woman, but the common people looked to me. Well, they should have me. For nearly fifty weary years I have applied ~~my mind to being Queen, and~~ the day I became Queen I buried my heart and with it my feelings. ~~I thought as England~~—I spoke and lived as England—~~I am England.~~ If ever I had any hopes or plans they ~~are forgotten~~—gone with my youth. The years have given me something in return—~~courage, will-power~~ ~~to endure and overcome the troubles that beset my undertaking~~—yes, and a pride in the achievement. But of serenity—love—happiness, I know nothing.

(*A pause* KATHERINE *bows her head*)

KATHERINE. Madam, I am ashamed of what I've said and done. (~~*She looks up pleadingly*~~) ~~I will never again~~ . . .
ELIZABETH. Do not be ashamed. You were thoughtless, ~~perhaps,~~ but you had t~~he courage and~~ a singleness of purpose which enabled you to do the thing you wished to do. ~~That same courage will give you strength to rise above vain and useless longings for things you cannot attain.~~ England isn't ready for women players yet. One day —who knows? Perhaps our spirit will be carried on and live again in future generations of women—the women who will lead fuller lives —~~who will have learnt to apply their intelligence and use their influence in the spheres that are open to them~~—in helping to guide the world from chaos and violence into serenity and peace.

(*There is a pause*)

~~Good night, my child~~—go to your rest. Remember ~~always that~~ I see and hear, and ~~that~~ I wish for nothing but good for my children.

(KATHERINE *kneels and kisses the Queen's hand*)

KATHERINE. God bless and keep Your Majesty.

(*She rises, curtsies, backs up* R, *turns, and exits quickly.* ELIZABETH *remains seated for a moment. Then she slowly rises and goes to the window,*

*looking out. In the distance a clock chimes the hour. She is again in the
shadow, only her face being revealed by the moonlight. She speaks softly*)

ELIZABETH. England! My child! My life! Keep my spirit alive,
and my children shall never perish.

The CURTAIN *descends very slowly as* ELIZABETH *remains motionless.*

THE PROVOK'D WIFE

By Sir John Vanbrugh

Lady Brute, young and attractive, tires of her middle-aged, surly, brutish husband, and she and her niece, Bellinda, court two gallants, Constant and Heartfree. Sir John Brute meets them, but does not recognize them, as the ladies are disguised; later he returns in a drunken state, and they contrive to deceive him.

Scene—*Sir John Brute's house.*
Time—*1697.*

Lady Brute (*indicates Sir John, her drunken husband, who is fast asleep and snoring*) So; thanks to Kind Heaven, he's fast for some hours.

Bellinda. 'Tis well he is so, for we must lie like the Devil to bring ourselves off.

Lady Brute. What shall we say, Bellinda?

Bellinda (*musing*) I'll tell you: it must all light upon Heartfree and I. We'll say he has courted me sometime, but for reasons unknown to us, has ever been very earnest the thing must be kept from Sir John. That therefore, hearing him upon the stairs, he ran into the closet, tho' against our will, and Constant with him to prevent Jealousy. And to give this a good Impudent face of Truth (that I may deliver you from the trouble you are in :) I'll e'en (if he pleases) Marry him.

Lady Brute. I'm beholden to you Cousin: but that would be carrying the Jest a little too far for your own sake: you know he's a Younger Brother, and has Nothing.

Bellinda. 'Tis true; but I like him, and have Fortune enough to keep above Extremity: I can't say I would live with him in a Cell upon Love and Bread and Butter. But I had rather have the Man I love, and a Middle State of Life, than that Gentleman in the chair there and twice your Ladyship's Splendour.

Lady Brute. In truth, you are in the Right on't: for I am very Uneasie with my Ambition. But perhaps had I married as you'll do, I might have been as ill us'd.

Bellinda. Some Risque, I do confess, there always is; but if a man has the least spark either of Honour or good Nature; he can never use a woman ill that loves him and makes his Fortune both. Yet I must own to you, some little Struggling I still have, with this teasing Ambition of ours. For Pride, you know, is as Natural to a Woman as 'tis to a Saint. I can't help being Fond of the Rogue; and

90

yet it goes to my Heart to think I must never Whisk to Hide-Park, with above a Pair of Horses; have no Coronet upon my Coach, nor a Page to carry up my Train. But above all—that business of Place —Well, taking Place is a noble Prerogative.

LADY BRUTE. Especially after a Quarrel.

BELLINDA. Or of a Rival. But pray say no more on't, for fear I change my Mind. For o' my Conscience, were't not for Your Affair in the ballance, I should go near to pick up some Odious Man of Quality yet, and only take poor Heartfree for a Gallant.

LADY BRUTE. Then him you must have, however things go?

BELLINDA. Yes.

LADY BRUTE. Why, we may pretend what we will; but 'tis a hard matter to Live without the Man we Love.

BELLINDA. Especially when we are married to the Man we Hate. Pray tell me? Do the Men of the Town ever believe us Virtuous, when they see us do so?

LADY BRUTE. O, no; Nor indeed, hardly, let us do what we will. They most of 'em think there is no such thing as Virtue consider'd in the strictest notion of it. And therefore when you hear 'em say, Such a one is a Woman of Reputation, They only mean she's a Woman of Discretion. For they Consider we have no more Religion than they have, nor so much Morality; and between you and I, Bellinda, I'm afraid the want of Inclinations seldom protects any of us.

BELLINDA. But what think you of the fear of being found out?

LADY BRUTE. I think that never kept any Woman virtuous long. We are not such cowards neither. No: Let us once pass fifteen, and we have so good an Opinion of our own Cunning, to believe the World can penetrate into what we would keep a secret, And so in short, We cannot reasonably blame the Men for judging of us by themselves.

BELLINDA. But sure we are not so Wicked as they are, after all?

LADY BRUTE. We are as Wicked, child, but our Vice lies another way: Men have more courage than we, so they commit more bold, Impudent Sins. They Quarrel, Fight, Swear, Drink, Blaspheme, and the Like. Whereas we, being Cowards, only Backbite, tell Lyes, Cheat at Cards and so forth. But 'tis late. Let's end our Discourse for tonight, and out of an excess of Charity, take a small Care of that nasty, drunken thing there. . . . Do but look at him, Bellinda.

BELLINDA. Ah . . . tis a Savoury Dish.

LADY BRUTE. As savoury as 'tis, I'm cloy'd with'it. Prithee, call the Butler to take it away.

BELLINDA. Call the Butler? . . . Call the Scavenger. (*She calls to a servant*) Who's there? Call Rasor! Let him take away his master, Scower him clean with a little Soap and Sand, and so put him to Bed.

LADY BRUTE. Come, Bellinda, I'll e'en lie with you tonight; and in the Morning we'll send for our Gentlemen to—set this matter even.

BELLINDA. With all my heart.

LADY BRUTE. Good night, my dear. (*Low curtsy*)

BELLINDA. G . . . Ha, ha, ha. (*Exeunt*)

PYGMALION

By George Bernard Shaw

Professor Higgins claims that he can pass off Eliza Doolittle as a duchess after a few months, and Mrs Pearce, his housekeeper, is given the task of scrubbing the grimy, Cockney flower girl.

Scene—*The spare bedroom of Henry Higgins's house.*
Time—*Early twentieth century.*

Eliza (*heard off stage, the sound getting nearer*) . . . and I don't owe 'm nothing, and I don't care; and I won't be put upon, and I have my feelings the same as anyone else. . . .

(Mrs Pearce, *the housekeeper, shows Eliza into the spare room*)

Mrs Pearce. I will have to put you here. This will be your bedroom.

Liza. Oh . . . h! I couldn't sleep 'ere, missus. It's too good for the likes of me. I should be afraid to touch anything. I ain't a duchess yet, you know.

Mrs Pearce. You have got to make yourself as clean as the room: then you won't be afraid of it. And you must call me Mrs Pearce, not missus.

(Mrs Pearce *opens the door leading into a bathroom*)

Liza (*entering*) Gawd! What's this? Is this where you wash clothes? Funny sort of a copper I call it.

Mrs Pearce. It is not a copper. This is where we wash ourselves, Eliza, and where I am going to wash you.

Liza. You expect me to get into that and wet meself all over. Not me! I should catch my death. I knew a woman did it every Saturday night, and she died of it.

Mrs Pearce. Mr Higgins has the gentlemen's bathroom downstairs and he has a bath every morning, in cold water.

Liza. Ugh! He's made of iron, that man!

Mrs Pearce. If you are to sit with him and the colonel and be taught you will have to do the same. They won't like the smell of you if you don't. But you can have the water as hot as you like. There are two taps: hot and cold.

Liza (*weeping*) I couldn't. I dursn't. It's not natural! It would kill me. I've never had a bath in me whole life: not what you'd call a proper one.

Mrs Pearce. Well, don't you want to be clean and sweet and

decent like a lady? You know you can't be a nice girl inside if you're a dirty slut outside.

LIZA. Booohooo!

MRS PEARCE. Now, stop crying and get back into your room, and take off all your clothes. Then wrap yourself in this (*takes wrapper*) and come back to me. I will get the bath ready.

LIZA (*all tears*) I can't. I won't. I'm not used to it. I've never took off all me clothes before. It's not right: it's not decent.

MRS PEARCE. Nonsense, child. Don't you take off all your clothes every night when you go to bed?

LIZA (*amazed*) No. Why should I? I should catch my death. Of course I take off my skirt.

MRS PEARCE. Do you mean that you sleep in the underclothes you wear in the daytime?

LIZA. What else have I to sleep in?

MRS PEARCE. You will never do that again as long as you live here. I will get you a proper nightdress.

LIZA. Do you mean change into cold things and lay awake shivering 'alf the night? You want to kill me, you do.

MRS PEARCE. I want to change you from a frowsy slut into a clean, respectable girl fit to sit with the gentlemen in the study. Are you going to trust me and do what I tell you or be thrown out and sent back to your flower basket?

LIZA. But you don't know what the cold is to me. You don't know how I dread it.

MRS PEARCE. Your bed won't be cold here: I will put a hot-water bottle in it. (*She pushes her into the bedroom*) Off with you and undress.

LIZA. Oh, if only I'd'a known what a dreadful thing it is to be clean I'd never a come. I didn't know when I was well off. I . . .

(MRS PEARCE *pushes her off and puts on a pair of rubber gloves, fills the bath, tests it with a bath thermometer. Perfumes the water, then takes a formidable looking long-handled scrubbing brush.*

Enter ELIZA, *huddled in the wrapper, a piteous spectacle of abject terror*)

MRS PEARCE. Now come along. Take that thing off.

LIZA. Oh, I couldn't, Mrs Pearce: I really couldn't. I never done such a thing.

MRS PEARCE. Nonsense. Here: step in and tell me whether it's hot enough for you.

LIZA. Ah . . . oo! Ah-ooo! It's too hot!

MRS PEARCE (*deftly snatching the gown away and throwing Eliza down on her back*) It won't hurt you. (*She sets to work on Eliza with the scrubbing brush*)

ELIZA'S *screams are heartrending.*

QUALITY STREET

by J. M. BARRIE

Phœbe Throssel feels she has grown too old to attract the handsome Captain Valentine Brown, who has returned, after ten years, from the Napoleonic Wars. When Phœbe dresses up to look young again, he believes her to be Miss Livvy, a niece of Phœbe and her elder sister, Susan. He gives them two tickets for the Ball, where Miss Livvy is an immediate success.

SCENE—*At the Ball.*
TIME—*Early nineteenth century.*

PHŒBE. Susan, drink this, I left it for you on purpose. I have such awful information to impart. Drink!

(PHŒBE *goes up* R, *peeps off, to see if the coast is clear—and comes down* C, *to Susan.* SUSAN *drinks tremblingly, and puts the glass on the table* LC)

(*Moving to* R *of Susan*) Oh, Susan, Miss Henrietta and Miss Fanny are here.

SUSAN (*looking at Phœbe*) Here?

PHŒBE (*nodding*) Suddenly my eyes lighted on them. At once I slipped to the ground.

SUSAN (*taking a pace to Phœbe*) You think they did not see you?

PHŒBE. I am sure of it. They talked for a moment to Ensign Blades, and then turned and seemed to be going towards the shrubbery.

SUSAN. He had told them you were there with Captain Brown.

PHŒBE. I was not. (*Half ashamed, yet gleeful*) But I was only waiting until Charlotte came back with my cloak. Oh, sister, I am sure they suspect, else why should they be here? They never go to balls.

(*Both walk up and down the stage excitedly*)

SUSAN. They have suspected for a week. Ever since they saw you in your veil, Phœbe, on the night of the first ball. How could they but suspect when they have visited us every day since then and we have always pretended that Livvy has gone out.

PHŒBE. Should they see me it will be idle to attempt to deceive them. (*She turns up* R)

SUSAN. Idle indeed! Phœbe—the scandal! You—a demure schoolmistress. (*She sits* C)

PHŒBE (*moving down* R, *distressed*) That is it, sister. A little happiness has gone to my head like strong waters. (*She moves restlessly across to* LC)

SUSAN. My dear, stand still, and think.

(PHŒBE *turns*)

PHŒBE. I dare not—I cannot! Oh, Susan, if they see me we need not open school again! (*She kneels* L *of Susan*) Oh, Susan. I know not what I am saying, but you know who it is that has turned me into this wild creature . . . (*She sobs*)

SUSAN. Oh, Valentine Brown—how could you!

PHŒBE (*raising her head and turning away*) To weary of Phœbe—to turn from her with a "Bah, you make me old . . ." and become enamoured in a night of a thing like this! (*She indicates herself*)

SUSAN. Yes, yes, indeed. (*Then, touching Phœbe with sympathy*) Yet he has been kind to us. He has been to visit us several times.

PHŒBE (*rising*) In the hope that he would see *her!* (*Facing Susan,* LC) Was he not most silent and gloomy when we always said she was gone out.

SUSAN. He is infatuate.

(PHŒBE *turns away weeping.* SUSAN *hesitates. Then*)

Sister, you are not partial to him still?

PHŒBE. No, Susan, no. (*She comes to* C *and sits* L *of Susan*) I did love him all those years, though I never spoke of it to you. I never had any hope—I put that away at once, I folded it up and kissed it and put it away like a pretty garment I could never wear again, but I loved to think of him as a noble man. (*She rises, scornfully and goes down* R) But he is not a noble man, and Livvy found it out in an hour. (*She turns*) The Gallant! (*Crossing up* LC, *almost exultantly*) I flirted that I might enjoy his fury. (*Turning to Susan*) Susan, there has been a declaration in his eyes all tonight, and when he cries: "Adorable Miss Livvy, be mine!" I mean to answer with an "Oh, la, how ridiculous you are! You are much too old—I have been but quizzing you, sir!"

SUSAN. Phœbe, how can you be so cruel?

PHŒBE (*to* C) Because he has taken from me the one great glory that is in a woman's life. Not a man's love—she can do without that —but her own dear, sweet love for him. He is unworthy of my love, and that is why I can be so cruel.

SUSAN. Oh, dear.

PHŒBE (*to above the chair* R *of the* LC *table*) And now my triumph is to be denied me, for we must steal away home now before Henrietta and Fanny see us.

SUSAN (*rising, and coming forward a little—eagerly*) Yes—yes!

PHŒBE (*sadly*) And tomorrow we must say that Livvy has gone back to her father, for I dare keep up this deception no longer.

(*The band is heard, playing very softly*)

Come, Susan. (*She moves up towards the* C *opening*)

SUSAN (*with a gesture to check Phœbe*) Those gentlemen would not let you go. Not that way . . .

(SUSAN *goes to the opening* R, *sees Fanny, off stage, and starts back.* PHŒBE *sees this and comes down a little*)

PHŒBE (C) What is it?

SUSAN (*turning, agitated*) Miss Fanny—she is coming here.

(SUSAN *signs to Phœbe. They both turn and run to the* L *exit*—PHŒBE *first—but she starts back*)

PHŒBE (L, *distressed*) Susan—'tis Henrietta!

SUSAN (LC, *panic-stricken*) We are lost!

PHŒBE (*coming down* L) Sit down quickly.

REBECCA

By Daphne du Maurier

The forbidding and malicious Mrs Danvers, housekeeper of Manderley, was devoted to Maxim de Winter's late wife, Rebecca, and resents the arrival of the young, inexperienced second Mrs de Winter.

Scene—*The Hall of Manderley, Maxim de Winter's country seat.*
Time—*1940.*

Mrs de Winter (rc, *near the coffee-stool*) How do you do?

Mrs Danvers. Good evening, madam. (*At the foot of the stairs*)

Mrs de Winter. You are Mrs Danvers, of course. Mr de Winter has told me about you. He said you—you are a very wonderful person, you do so much for Manderley.

(Mrs Danvers *doesn't reply.* Mrs de Winter *struggles on, at a loss for words*)

It all seems very big to me, you know. You will have to show me round when you are not too busy.

Mrs Danvers. It's for you to make your own time, madam. (*She crosses to below the left end of the settee*)

(Mrs de Winter *looks taken aback by Mrs Danver's manner*)

Of course I don't know what you and Mr de Winter have arranged. The house has been in my charge now for nearly a year, and Mr de Winter has never complained. It was very different when the late Mrs de Winter was alive . . . there was a lot of entertaining then, and she liked to supervise things herself.

Mrs de Winter (*quickly*) You must run the house as it has always been run. I don't want to make any changes.

Mrs Danvers. Very good, madam. Then I can give orders for things to continue as usual. Breakfast in the dining-room at nine, and the fire lit in the morning-room when cold. Mrs de Winter always did her correspondence in the morning-room after breakfast. On cold days the fire is lit here in the afternoon just before tea. If you wish it lit earlier, I will give orders for it to be done.

Mrs de Winter. Oh, no. I'm sure I shan't need it any earlier.

Mrs Danvers. Alice is unpacking for you now and will look after you until your maid arrives.

Mrs de Winter (*awkwardly*) I haven't got a maid.

Mrs Danvers. It's usual, madam, you know, for ladies in your position, to have a personal maid.

MRS DE WINTER. If—if you think it's necessary, perhaps you would see about it for me.

MRS DANVERS. Just as you wish. It's for you to say, madam.

MRS DE WINTER. Thank you.

(*She knocks against the stool.* MRS DANVERS *crosses, picks up the glass from the stool and puts it on the tray on the table*)

Thank you. I suppose you have been here at Manderley for many years, longer than anyone else?

MRS DANVERS. Not so long as Frith. Frith was here when Mr de Winter was a boy.

MRS DE WINTER. Oh! really. So you didn't come till after that?

MRS DANVERS (*pause*) I came here when the late Mrs de Winter was a bride. (*She looks at her with a curious mixture of pity and scorn*)

MRS DE WINTER (*shocked, a little scared*) Oh! . . . Oh, I see.

(*Another long pause*)

MRS DANVERS (*speaking a little faster than hitherto*) If Mr de Winter doesn't like the arrangement of the new wing, he must tell me.

MRS DE WINTER. I had no idea Mr de Winter was having anything changed. He shouldn't have done it—for me.

MRS DANVERS. Mr de Winter said he would prefer it.

MRS DE WINTER. Oh! Do we see the sea from our rooms?

MRS DANVERS. No. And from your wing you can't even hear it, either. You wouldn't know the sea was anywhere near, not from your wing. (*Her manner is peculiar*)

MRS DE WINTER (*senses it*) I'm sorry about that. I like the sea.

(*A pause*)

MRS DANVERS (*she watches Mrs de Winter intently*) They used to live in the west wing when Mrs de Winter was alive, but those rooms haven't been used since she was drowned. (*A pause. In a bright, hard voice*) Would you like me to show you your rooms?

MRS DE WINTER. I think perhaps I'd rather wait till Mr de Winter comes back. He said he wouldn't be long. (*She glances half-heartedly towards the window and the terrace*)

MRS DANVERS (*moving to the foot of the stairs*) Very good, madam.

MRS DE WINTER (*rather desperately crosses to Mrs Danvers*) Mrs Danvers, I hope we shall be friends. This sort of life is new to me. And I do want to make a success of it, and above all to make Mr de Winter happy. You will help me, won't you?

MRS DANVERS. I shall try and see that everything runs smoothly, madam. Naturally, it is a little difficult for me and the rest of the staff. We were all very devoted to the late Mrs de Winter.

MRS DE WINTER (*her voice almost a whisper*) Yes—I understand.

MRS DANVERS. When we heard that Mr de Winter was to marry again, we could hardly believe it at first, but Mr Crawley explained to us how it was. He said he supposed the empty house had got on

Mr de Winter's nerves, and he could not go on living here alone. (*There is a world of malice behind the words*) If there is nothing more at present, I will go and see if Alice has finished unpacking your clothes. Dinner is at eight o'clock. (*She turns to mount the stairs*) Good night, madam.

MRS DE WINTER. Good night.

THE RECRUITING OFFICER

By George Farquhar

*Silvia, a forthright generous girl, returns to her home town, Shrewsbury, where
Captain Plume, the man she loves, is recruiting soldiers for the army. She
visits her coquettish cousin, Melinda, a lady of fortune.*

Scene—*Melinda's apartment.*
Time—*1705.*

Melinda. Welcome to town, Cousin Silvia. I envied you your
retreat in the country, for Shrewsbury, methinks, and all your heads
of shires are the most irregular places for living. Here we have
smoke, noise, scandal, affectation, and pretension, in short, everything to give the spleen and nothing to divert it. Then the air is
intolerable.

Silvia. Oh, madam, I have heard the town commended for its
air.

Melinda. But you don't consider, Silvia, how long I have lived
in it; for, I can assure you that to a lady the least nice in her constitution, no air can be good above half a year. Change of air I take
to be most agreeable of any variety in life.

Silvia. As you say, Cousin Melinda, there are several sorts of airs:
airs in conversation, airs in behaviour, airs in dress. Then we have
our quality airs, our sickly airs, our reserved airs, and sometimes our
impudent airs.

Melinda. Pshaw, I talk only of the air we breathe, or more
properly, of that we taste. Have not you, Silvia, found a vast difference in the taste of airs?

Silvia. Pray, Cousin, are not vapours a sort of air? Taste air?
You may as well tell me I might feed upon air. But prithee, my dear
Melinda, don't put on such airs to me. Your education and mine
were just the same, and I remember the time when we never troubled
our heads about air, but when the sharp air from the Welsh moun-
tains made our noses drop in a cold morning at the boarding school.

Melinda. Our education, Cousin, was the same, but our tem-
peraments had nothing alike. You have the constitution of a horse.

Silvia. So far as to be troubled with neither spleen colic nor
vapours. I need no salt for my stomach, no hartshorn for my head,
nor wash for my complexion. I can gallop all the morning after the
hunting horn, and all the evening after a fiddle. In short I can do
everything with my father but drink and shoot flying, and I'm sure
I can do everything my mother could were it put to the trial.

MELINDA. You are in a fair way of being put to't, for I am told your captain is come to town.

SILVIA. Ay, Melinda, he is come, and I'll take care he shan't go without a companion.

MELINDA. You're certainly mad, Cousin.

SILVIA. And there's a pleasure sure, in being mad. Which none but madmen know.

MELINDA. Thou poor romantic, Quixote. Hast thou the vanity to imagine that a young, sprightly officer that rambles over half the globe in half a year can confine his thoughts to the little daughter of a country justice in an obscure corner of the world?

SILVIA. Pshaw! What care I for his thoughts? I should not like a man with confined thoughts; it shows a narrowness of soul. Constancy is but a dull, sleepy quality at best; they will hardly admit it among the manly virtues. Nor do I think it deserves a place with bravery, knowledge, policy, justice, and some other qualities that are proper to that noble sex. In short, Melinda, I think a petticoat a mighty simple thing, and I'm heartily tired of my sex.

MELINDA. That is, you are tired of an appendix to our sex that you can't so handsomely get rid of in petticoats as if you were in breeches. O' my conscience, Silvia, hadst thou been a man, thou hadst been the greatest rake in Christendom.

SILVIA. I should endeavour to know the world, which a man can never do thoroughly without half a hundred friendships and as many amours. But now I think on't, how stands your affair with Mr Worthy?

MELINDA. He's my aversion.

SILVIA. Vapours!

MELINDA. What do you say, madam?

SILVIA. I say that you should not use that honest fellow so inhumanely. He's a gentleman of parts and fortune, and beside that he's my Plume's friend, and by all that's sacred, if you don't use him better I shall expect satisfaction.

MELINDA. Satisfaction! You begin to fancy yourself in breeches in good earnest. But to be plain with you, I like Worthy the worse for being so intimate with your captain, for I take him to be a loose, idle, unmannerly coxcomb!

SILVIA. Oh, madam. You never saw him, perhaps, since you were mistress of twenty thousand pound. You only knew him when you were capitulating with Worthy for a settlement which might encourage him to be a little loose and unmannerly with you.

MELINDA. What do you mean, madam?

SILVIA. My meaning needs no interpretation, madam.

MELINDA. Better it had, madam, for methinks you're too plain.

SILVIA. If you mean the plainness of my person, I think your ladyship as plain as me to the full.

MELINDA. Were I assured of that I should be glad to take up with a rakely officer as you do.

SILVIA. Again! Look 'e, madam, you're in your own house.

MELINDA. And if you had kept in yours I should have excused you.

SILVIA. Don't be troubled, madam. I shan't desire to have my visit returned.

MELINDA. The sooner therefore you make an end of this, the better.

SILVIA. I'm easily advised to follow my inclinations. So, madam, your humble servant.

MELINDA. Saucy thing!

THE RELUCTANT DEBUTANTE

By William Douglas Home

Sheila and Jimmy Broadbent have rented a flat for the London season for their daughter Jane's "coming out". Sheila is anxious to find the right partner for her daughter, but Jane is very casual and bored with most of the suggested escorts.

Scene—*The Broadbents' London flat, off Eaton Square, London.*
Period—*Modern.*

(Sheila Broadbent *is dialling a number.* Jane *is at the breakfast table*)

SHEILA. Good-bye, darling. And don't be late. Remember about Mabel. . . .

JANE. Mummy . . .

SHEILA. Yes, what is it, darling?

JANE. Daddy's gone.

SHEILA. Yes, darling, I expect he has. Why, did you want him?

JANE. No, but couldn't you stop talking to him when he isn't here?

SHEILA (*on the telephone.* JANE *drinks orange juice, and glances at letters*) Hullo? Mabel? Darling, yes, it is. Mabel, darling. Tell me, who was that young man Clarissa danced the fox-trot with last night? Which one? Well, the one where Lady Price fell down. I know, my dear . . . poor Harold really ought to keep an eye on her. I know. Too dangerous for words. My dear . . . and did you see the French Ambassador? He had to literally hurdle her with Eileen Privett in his arms. I know, and she's no midget is she? Yes, poor man, I do hope that he hasn't strained his heart. Well, Mabel, what did I ring up about? Oh, yes, of course—Jane says his name is David. I don't know. I'll ask her. (*To Jane*) Darling, Mabel says do you mean David Bulloch?

JANE. Ask her if he's goofy looking.

SHEILA (*at the telephone*) Jane says is he goofy looking? (*To Jane*) Yes, a little, dear. (*At the telephone*) No, no, of course it doesn't matter. Do you know where I can get hold of him? Yes, please do, Mabel—that's too kind of you. (*To Jane*) She's sent Clarissa up to get her book. (*At the telephone*) Yes, wasn't it too lovely? Did you? Oh, how sweet of you. I simply must tell her at once. (*To* JANE *who is leaving the trolley with scrambled eggs*) Jane darling, Mabel says you looked too wonderful for words last night.

(JANE *puts out her tongue*)

She's thrilled. And what about Clarissa? Did she like it? I'm so glad. I thought that she was looking simply radiant. She is so sensible, not dancing all the time. Oh, has she?... Oh, I see, her shoe's been rubbing her, poor thing! Oh, Mabel, by the way, who was that very dark young man Clarissa danced a waltz with? Sunburn, was it? David Hoylake-Johnston. Where's he come from? Oh, two years? The lucky boy. I always think Majorca's too divine! Oh, Malaya!—poor dear boy—not so dear! But what do you mean, Mabel? If he's not all right, why did you let Mabel dance with him?

(JANE *goes to the trolley with cup and saucer. Inspects the coffee*)

No, I suppose you couldn't if they met at dinner. No—no—Mabel —no! (*To Jane*) Jane—run into the kitchen and ask Mrs Edgar for some more hot milk.

JANE. There's lots here.

SHEILA. It's cold surely, darling.

JANE (*pouring*) That won't matter. There's no coffee left.

SHEILA (*putting down the cup, picks up the coffee-pot*) Jane, do as you're told.

(JANE *goes out with the coffee-pot.* SHEILA *at the telephone again*)

Yes, Mabel, do go on. I've sent Jane to the kitchen. Oh, my dear, so that's why Brenda Barrington went off to ski in May. He was the man. But didn't you just say that he was in Malaya? Oh, I see, his leave had started then. I know, my dear. That always seems to make them so impetuous.

(JANE *returns*)

Well, Mabel, till tonight and you must tell me all. (*She hangs up*) Oh, bother. I haven't got the number now!

(JANE *pours coffee*)

JANE. It serves you right. You shouldn't gossip so.

SHEILA. But, darling, I was doing it for you.

JANE. I don't want David Bulloch for a partner, thank you.

SHEILA. Why not, darling. Mabel says he's charming.

JANE. Everybody knows he's goofy.

SHEILA. Nonsense, Jane. Now. What was Mabel's number?

JANE. I've forgotten.

(SHEILA *goes to the telephone book*)

You're only asking him because he's going to be a peer.

SHEILA. A what?

JANE. A peer. You know what peers are, Mummy. David's going to be Lord Cirencester.

SHEILA (*feigning ignorance*) Who told you, Jane?

JANE. He did.

SHEILA. How very vulgar he must be.

JANE. Well, it's no more than someone saying he's going to be an engine driver.

SHEILA. No-one ever says that, darling.

JANE. I expect engine drivers do.

SHEILA. When they've been asked perhaps. I hope you didn't ask him, darling.

JANE. No, he told me straight out of the blue—just like you might say, "Jane is coming out this year," he said, "I'll be Lord Ciren-cester one day actually."

SHEILA. And what did you say?

JANE. I said it couldn't bore me more.

SHEILA. How very rude.

JANE. He quite agreed. He said it couldn't bore me more than it bored him.

SHEILA (*she has found the number*) Oh, did he, darling? He sounds fun. Sloane seven-three-eight-one. We really ought to write it down somewhere.

JANE. I can't see why.

SHEILA. Well, darling, after all, Clarissa is your greatest friend.

JANE. She's not.

SHEILA. Of course she is.

JANE. She's all right in the country, but she's horrible in London.

SHEILA. Horrible! Of course she isn't.

JANE. Yes, she is. She's always giggling and looking sideways.

SHEILA. Nonsense, darling. That's just your imagination.

JANE. No, it's not. It's hers.

SHEILA. Engaged. (*She replaces the receiver*) Did you like any of the young men that you danced with last night, darling?

JANE. No.

SHEILA. You must have found some of them nicer than the others?

JANE. No, I didn't. They were all the same.

SHEILA. Darling, how absurd. No two people are the same.

JANE. They are.

SHEILA. What did they talk to you about?

JANE. Oh, Ascot, Wimbledon and Goodwood. And the dance the night before, and then the dance the next night. It's so boring I could scream.

SHEILA. But you like dancing, don't you?

JANE. Not with them.

SHEILA. Why not.

JANE. They're all so young.

SHEILA. You mean they don't dance properly?

JANE. Oh, yes, they do. That's just what's wrong. They couldn't dance more properly.

SHEILA. Darling, what do you mean?

JANE. Oh, Mummy, you know quite well what I mean. They

dance just like two people going for a walk except that you're walking backwards. Well, that's not what dancing's for. I mean when natives dance a love dance out in Africa, it means something.

SHEILA. Oh! What does it mean, darling?

JANE. Well, they're making love.

SHEILA. Jane!

JANE. I don't mean literally. It's in the early stages still.

SHEILA (*relieved*) Oh.

JANE. But they're hotting up for it. That's why they do it. Otherwise they wouldn't do it. They'd go for a walk instead.

SHEILA. But, darling, they're primitive.

JANE. Well, love is primitive.

SHEILA. Oh, is it, darling?

JANE. That's just what I like about them. They're honest and we aren't. They know what dancing's for. And if it's not for that, it's not for anything. . . . What are you laughing at?

SHEILA. Oh, nothing. (*She laughs again*) I just had a vision of your father bounding up and down in feathers in the River Room.

JANE. Well, it'd do him much more good than propping up the bar.

SHEILA. There I agree.

JANE. I knew you would.

SHEILA. Only about Daddy, darling. I still disagree in principle. I must try Mabel for that young man's number now. (*Going to the telephone*) Just think! I danced with two M.P.s last night, one minister, two colonels and the air attaché from the Swedish Embassy. Well, if one only danced as a preliminary to making love, my goodness! I wouldn't have much reputation left this morning, would I? (*On the phone*) Oh, Mabel darling, we were cut off. It's too annoying, isn't it? Now, Mabel, did Clarissa get the . . . Oh, how kind of you! (*To Jane*) Write it down. And stop picking your nose. (*On the telephone*) No, Mabel, don't be silly. I was talking to Jane. You were, too? What a strange coincidence. Yes, yes, I'm ready. (*To Jane*) Now, darling, write it down. Yes? Mayfair six-three-eight-four. Thank you so much.

(JANE *writes with the fork on the tablecloth*)

What's that? Eileen? In the London Clinic! Strained her what? My dear, I do hope the French Ambassador's all right. I just can't wait to hear.

JANE. Gossip . . . gossip . . . gossip!

A ROOM IN THE TOWER

By Hugh Stewart

The young Lady Jane Grey, imprisoned in the Tower of London after her short reign, is visited by the new Queen, her cousin, Mary Tudor.

SCENE—*A room in the Tower of London.*
TIME—*1554.*

MARY. Cousin Jane?
JANE. I am Jane Grey.
MARY (*after a pause*) You have changed.

> (MARY *advances, carefully because of her high heels. The door is closed*)

(*Considering her*) The daughter of my Duke of Suffolk. . . . I had not thought of my cousin like this. Quite beautiful, too! (*She laughs*) It's strange, our family has rarely been famed for good looks before. You may sit. Which relative is it who has been so generous? Not your father, surely?
JANE. You are pleased to jest, madam.
MARY. Tush! No doubt those charms are responsible for your fame. We can see our Lords have acted wisely; what hope have I against such a creature? Men are so susceptible to fine features.
JANE (*protesting*) You are laughing at me. . . .
MARY. Troy was laid waste for Helen.
JANE. Have you no feeling?
MARY. Come, madam, I'm sorry to have to see you in such a place as this. You have been moved from the King's House?
JANE (*in a low voice*) Yes. Does that mean . . . that it will be soon now?
MARY. I know nothing about it.
JANE. This window directly overlooks the place. Is that so that I can . . . prepare myself?
MARY (*frowns*) I shall see that you are removed within a few days. Is that your wish?
JANE. It is my wish.
MARY. Very well, I shall instruct the lieutenant. Were you happy in Leicestershire?
JANE. When I was learning; Doctor Aylmer was so patient and gentle. He made life seem so much more to me.
MARY. Your tutor?
JANE. Yes, madam.
MARY. We have heard of your great learning, Jane.

JANE. My father gave great care to my education.

MARY. Like my own, I think that is all I have to thank him for. He was very proud of my achievements. You speak in Latin, and Greek?

JANE. Oh, yes, I love them dearly.

MARY (*indicating the table*) What are these papers here?

JANE. Some Hebrew I have been studying.

MARY. Hebrew too! (*Examining the papers*) Do you know the tongue?

JANE. I wish I knew it better.

MARY. I see you write in Arabic.

JANE. A little, madam.

MARY. My mother was my first teacher in Latin. When I was nine I replied in that tongue to the commissioners sent from Flanders. I can see the King now . . . how proud he was. . . . (*She sighs*) Have you repented, child?

JANE. Have I sinned, madam?

MARY. Why are you here?

JANE. Because of man's ambition.

MARY. You answer with a brief tongue.

JANE. Oh, madam, can you think it was my own desire so far to reach above myself? Indeed, I dared not of my own accord. Such a position held nothing but terror for me.

MARY. I can believe you.

JANE. All that I could ask from life . . .

MARY. What is that?

JANE. My husband's love, I think that is all.

MARY. A woman's life is one of sacrifice, and for such worthless men. You love Guildford Dudley?

JANE (*simply*) More than anyone in the world.

MARY. They say I should wed an English lord and I say I will not. We shall see! There is not one I could care for; I know them too well. They are perverse, pig-headed fools! Yet you say you still love this . . . this man. The traitor who usurped our throne and set aside our Divine Right, as something of less importance than his own pride.

JANE. That fatal pride.

MARY. It is fatal to oppose God's will; people have discovered that and many more will discover it in the future. There are things which must be accomplished and which I will accomplish . . . alone if need be. It is necessary to proceed cautiously now, but they will be done before I die. (*She turns to Jane*) Why did you plead guilty?

JANE. I am not very strong.

MARY. They dared to threaten you?

JANE. I was afraid, perhaps.

MARY. Was that all? Your father told you to plead guilty? Answer me!

JANE. Oh, madam . . .

MARY. Answer me!

JANE. I am guilty.

MARY. Do you know where your father is now?

JANE. What have you done to him?

MARY. Do you care?

JANE. He is dead?

MARY. He deserved to be hanged like a common footpad.

JANE. What have you done!

MARY. I cannot understand you, Jane. He is not worth a moment's anxiety. That is why I have spared him. He is such a fool; I think he has been frightened enough.

JANE. You have spared my father?

MARY. He was shown the dungeons, and he has seen a man on the rack. I would not stain my shoe to crush a worm under foot.

JANE (*on her knees*) Oh, God bless you! God bless you! Your mercy will be rewarded. (*Her voice faltering*) Madam, there is something . . .

MARY. Well?

JANE. If you think me bold, I am only made so by your exceeding goodness. It urges me to hope, to believe that you will extend your compassion to . . . to the Archbishop Cranmer . . .

(*The* QUEEN *starts*)

Oh, Cousin, I beseech you to spare the old man.

MARY. I must have no heart.

JANE. But you are not heartless, you are not. You have shown me how great it is.

MARY (*touched*) You are the first person to say that to me.

JANE. The Primate is old . . .

MARY. He is a traitor like the rest of you!

JANE. No, madam, he is not in entire possession of his strength. When he consented to my succession it was only after a long period in which he opposed it. He has given many years in devoted allegiance to the Crown. Oh, Cousin, don't dishonour him in his old age; he was worn down, he feared for his life . . . don't let them kill him!

MARY. They cannot, without my consent.

JANE. Then have mercy on him; let his gratitude be added to mine, I implore you.

MARY. I shall see no hurt comes to him; that is all I can promise now.

JANE. You promise that?

(MARY *nods*)

But you are the Sovereign.

MARY (*sadly*) I am only a woman, Jane. Ah, if I had been a man . . . everything would be so easy. I should command and dictate and make England glorious. I should throw off this heavy cloak of hypocrisy. I should be a slave to no living person only to God.

JANE (*softly*) Your people believe in you.

MARY. Do they? Do you think they do?

JANE. Yes.

MARY. But they don't understand. I am not a hard woman, and God knows my life has been hard. I must do these things if it breaks my heart. To restore our violated faith and unite, with bonds of steel, the two greatest countries in the world. That is my mission, and I have no wish to die with the certainty it has failed. (*To Jane*) In a few days you will leave this prison-house, for ever.

JANE (*quietly, after a pause*) I don't think I can die, as I ought to die, unless I see him again.

MARY. Your husband?

JANE. Yes. You see my life has been so empty; if there is no life after death . . . nothing, no afterwards . . . I . . . I couldn't bear it! It's all that I have left . . . that I will be with him in heaven.

MARY. My poor child, you need not be afraid.

JANE. I'm not really afraid, only . . . sometimes . . .

MARY. I mean you to go into life, not death.

JANE (*in a whisper*) Life!

MARY. I pardon you, Jane.

JANE. Into life! Both of us!

MARY. I am satisfied of your innocence.

JANE. Both of us?

MARY (*evading the question*) There is life waiting for you, full of sunshine, and joy, beautiful things . . . and children.

JANE. Oh, madam . . . madam! (*With shaking hands she raises the hem of the Queen's skirt to her lips*) My happiness . . . I can't express it. I feel . . . it's so great . . . it won't let me speak.

MARY (*tenderly*) I understand. There is no cause for you to kneel.

JANE. We shall pray for you and bless you . . . in every prayer of our lives.

MARY. Remember me, when you are happy, will you?

JANE. Always.

MARY. I shall need all your prayers. It is hard . . . it is so hard sometimes, to do my duty. I wish I were finished with it all, but I must go onwards. (*She rises*) Duty comes before everything. Everything. I must leave you. I have been too long already.

JANE. Must you . . . must you go?

MARY (*nods*) Duty compels me; it has been like that, always. Farewell. (*She moves away, and turns for a moment at the door*) Be wise, Jane. (*Off stage*) Your arm, my Lord, please, I tire so quickly now.

ROOTS

By Arnold Wesker

Beatie, twenty-two, a fervent, straightforward country girl, influenced by her free-thinking London boy friend, Ronnie, revisits her parents' cottage. Mrs Bryant, her mother, is a stout, brisk, seemingly aggressive woman of about fifty.

Scene—*Kitchen-living-room of the Bryants' cottage, Norfolk.*
Time—*The present.*

Mrs Bryant. You heard that Ma Buckley hev been taken to Mental Hospital in Norwich? Poor ole dear. If there's one thing I can't abide that's mental cases. They frighten me—they do. Can't face 'em. I'd sooner follow a man to a churchyard than the mental hospital. That's a terrible thing to see a person lose their reason—that 'tis. Well, I tell you what, down where I used to live, down the other side of the Hall, years ago we moved in next to an old woman. I only had Jenny and Frank then—an' this woman she were the sweetest of people. We used to talk and do errands for each other—Oh, she was a sweet ole dear. And then one afternoon I was going out to get my washin' in and I saw her. She was standin' in a tub o' water up to her neck. She was! Up to her neck. An' her eyes had that glazed, wonderin' look and she stared straight at me she did. Straight at me. Well, do you know what? I was struck *dumb*. I was *struck* dumb wi' shock. What wi' her bein' so nice all this while, the sudden comin' on her like that in the tub fair upset me. It did! And people tell me afterwards that she's bin goin' in an' out o' hospital for years. Blust, that scare me. That scare me so much she nearly took me round the bend wi' her.

(Beatie *appears from behind the curtain in her dressing-gown, a towel round her head*)

Beatie. There! I'm gonna hev a bath every day when I'm married.

(Beatie *starts rubbing her hair with the towel and fiddles with the radio. She finds a programme playing Mendelssoh's Fourth Symphony, the slow movement, and stands before the mirror, listening and rubbing*)

Beatie (*looking at her reflection*) Isn't your nose a funny thing, and your ears. And your arms and your legs, aren't they funny things—sticking out of a lump.

MRS BRYANT (*switching off the radio*) Turn that squit off!

BEATIE (*turning on her mother violently*) *Mother!* I could kill you when you do that. No wonder I don't know anything about anything. I never heard nothing but dance music because you always turned off the classics. I never knowed anything about the news because you always switched off after the headlines. I never read any good books 'cos there was never any in the house.

MRS BRYANT. What's gotten into you now, gal?

BEATIE. God in heaven, Mother, you live in the country but you got no—no—no majesty. You spend your time among green fields, you grow flowers and you breathe fresh air and you got no majesty. Your mind's cluttered up with nothing and you shut out the world. What kind of a life did you give me?

MRS BRYANT. Blust, gal, I weren't no teacher.

BEATIE. But you hindered. You didn't open one door for me. Even his mother cared more for me than what you did. Beatie, she say, Beatie, why don't you take up evening classes and learn something other than waitressing. Yes, she say, you won't ever regret learnin' things. But did you care what job I took up or whether I learned things? You didn't even think it was necessary.

MRS BRYANT. I fed you. I clothed you. I took you out to the sea. What more d'you want. We're only country folk you know. We ent got no big things here you know.

BEATIE. Squit! Squit! It makes no difference country or town. *All* the town girls I ever worked with were just like me. It makes no difference country or town—that's squit. Do you know when I used to work at the holiday camp and I sat down with the other girls to write a letter we used to sit and discuss what we wrote about. An' we all agreed, all on us, that we started: "Just a few lines to let you know", and then we get on to the weather and then we get struck so we write about each other and after a page an' half of big scrawl end up: "Hoping this finds you as well as it leaves me." There! We couldn't say any more. Thousands of things happening at this holiday camp and we couldn't find words for them. All of us the same, Hundreds of girls and one day we're gonna be mothers, and you *still* talk to me of Jimmy Skelton and the ole woman in the tub. Do you know I've heard that story a dozen times. A dozen times. Can't you hear yourself, Mother? Jesus, how can I bring Ronnie to this house.

MRS BRYANT. Blust, gal, if Ronnie don't like us then he . . .

BEATIE. Oh, he'll like you all right. He like people. He'd've loved ole Stan Mann. Ole Stan Mann would've understood everything Ronnie talk about. Blust! That man liked livin'. Besides, Ronnie say it's too late for the old 'uns to learn. But he says it's up to us young 'uns. And them of us that know hev got to teach them of us as don't know.

MRS BRYANT. I bet he hev a hard time trying to change you, gal!

BEATIE. He's *not* trying to change me, Mother. You can't change people, he say, you can only give them some love and hope they'll take it. And he's tryin' to teach me and I'm tryin' to understand—do you see that, Mother?

MRS BRYANT. I don't see what that's got to do with music though.

BEATIE. Oh, my God! (*Suddenly*) I'll show you. (*Goes off to the front room to collect pick-up and a record*) Now sit you down, gal, and I'll show you. Don't start ironing or reading or nothing, just sit there and be prepared to learn something. (*She appears with pick-up and switches on*) You aren't too old, just you sit and listen. That's the trouble, you see, we ent ever prepared to learn anything, we close our minds the minute anything unfamiliar appear. *I* could never listen to music. I used to like some on it but then I'd lose patience, I'd go to bed in the middle of a symphony, or my mind would wander 'cos the music didn't mean anything to me so I'd go to bed or start talking. "Sit back, woman," he'd say, "listen to it. Let it happen to you and you'll grow as big as the music itself."

MRS BRYANT. Blust he talk like a book.

BEATIE. An' sometimes he talk as though you didn't know where the moon or the stars was. (*She puts on a record of Bizet's "L'Arlésienne" Suite*) Now listen. This is a simple piece of music, it's not highbrow but it's full of living. And that's what he say socialism is. "Christ," he say. "Socialism isn't talking all the time, it's living, it's singing, it's dancing, it's being interested in what go on around you, it's being concerned about people and the world." Listen, Mother. (*She becomes breathless and excited*) Listen to it. It's simple, isn't it? Can you call that squit?

MRS BRYANT. I don't say it's all squit.

BEATIE. You don't have to frown because it's alive.

MRS BRYANT. No, not all on it's squit.

BEATIE. See the way the other tune comes in? Hear it? Two simple tunes, one after the other.

MRS BRYANT. I aren't sayihg it's all squit.

BEATIE. And now listen, listen, it goes together, the two tunes together, they knit, they're perfect. Don't it make you want to dance? (*She begins to dance a mixture of a cossack dance and a sailor's hornpipe*)

(*The music becomes fast and her spirits are young and high*)

Listen to that, Mother. Is it difficult? Is it squit? It's light. It make me feel light and confident and happy. God, Mother, we could all be so much more happy and alive. Wheeeee . . .

BEATIE *claps her hands and dances on and her* MOTHER *smiles and claps her hands and—*

the CURTAIN *falls*

A SCENT OF FLOWERS

by JAMES SAUNDERS

Zoe, a young girl, unhappy and in love with a married man, has committed suicide. During her funeral, scenes from her life are enacted. Agnes is her hard, sophisticated stepmother.

SCENE—*A room.*
TIME—*The present.*

ZOE. No . . . No, no, no . . . I can't, it's not possible . . . I can't do it. Do you think I'm *not* being realistic? My God, I've never before realized what it *meant*, to be realistic. You're the one who's not facing facts. You think there's still a way out. There isn't. When I lay awake at night, I used to tell myself, "Things will get better, things will look better in the morning." I don't any more, there isn't light and day for me any more, it's, it's . . . it's all the s-same . . . It's what they call the—dark night of the soul . . . And I'm—in it— all the time . . . Except for just a few minutes now and then when I'm in your arms and it—it goes . . . And then . . . I'm so used to this— feeling that when it goes for those few minutes it's—as though there's nothing left to take its place . . . as though I've died . . .

AGNES. Zoe, do you think we might have a talk?

(ZOE *looks round at her, with dull eyes. She inclines her head slightly*)

ZOE. What about? The weather? No?

AGNES. I would appreciate it, Zoe, if you could believe that I want to do something for you.

ZOE. Like what?

AGNES. I understand that you are—in difficulty.

ZOE. You *understand?* Do you?

AGNES. Zoe, I think you are old enough now to stop treating me as something out of a fairy tale.

ZOE. I don't know what you're talking about.

AGNES. We don't live in fairyland, Zoe; the world isn't divided into good fairies and bad fairies, or even good people and bad people. There are people we have to live with and people we don't. It's a very hard world, Zoe. There are no easy ways out. There are no allowances made for difficulties in our childhood. There are no enchanted castles we can escape to when our relationships get too difficult. There are people we have to live with and people we don't, and we have to do the best we can. I am not a wicked stepmother, I'm the woman your father married after he left your mother, and this fact has made it necessary for us to accept each other as people and try to understand each other and try to help each other.

ZOE. What a cold woman you are, Agnes.

AGNES. I try to understand, Zoe.

ZOE. You do everything in your head, don't you? You don't have any heart; have you ever loved *anyone?* How can you understand?

(*Pause.* DAVID *enters, stands apart, uncertainly*)

ZOE. Daddy . . . I'm in trouble . . . I'm in trouble, Daddy . . . (*Her voice is that of a terrified child locked in a dark room*)

AGNES. Zoe, will you listen to me!

(ZOE *looks at her with wide, empty eyes.* AGNES *bites her lip. Pause*)

I know what's happened.

ZOE. Really?

AGNES. I should like to try to help.

ZOE (*in the same tone as before*) Really? (*She holds herself very upright, as though keeping control of every muscle; her voice has a cold, ironical lightness*)

AGNES. I don't think you can afford any longer to choose where help is to come from.

(*Slight pause*)

I'm trying very hard to make some kind of contact so as to help you. I've stopped expecting anything but dislike from you, but you can at least assume that my intentions are good. There's a way out, Zoe, if you'll listen to me. I know what you're going through. But it's in yourself. Do you understand? It exists only in you. It isn't something apart from you. However beautiful and profound and important you think it is, it's no bigger than you are, because it's part of you and you're small, Zoe, like everyone else, small and insignificant. Zoe you've got to grow up very quickly. You've got to stand outside yourself for the first time in your life and see yourself in retrospect— an emotionally unbalanced child who's got herself into an affair with a married man. Just another. It's happened before. It happened to me. It's unimportant. Nobody gives a damn about it.

(*Pause*)

You've got to get it out of your system, Zoe.

(*Slight pause*)

You're only another immature child opening her legs to just another married man.

(ZOE *makes a sound, turns away, picks up the flowers*)

You have to make a decision. Why don't you stop playing the tragic soul at the mercy of the fates, and grow up. No-one's at the mercy of the fates unless they want to be. Make a decision, Zoe.

(ZOE *is facing the grille, looking down at the flowers*)

Do you understand what I'm saying!

(AGNES *grips her by the lower arm; ZOE cries out as though in pain, tears her arm away, and nurses it, her face contorted. The flowers have fallen to the ground. AGNES stares at her, and steps back*)

What have you done to your arm?

ZOE. Daddy—I'm in trouble . . .

(AGNES *shakes her head. DAVID is looking at Zoe, but doesn't move from his place. AGNES turns to him*)

AGNES. Why don't you do something?

Long tableau.

THE SERVANT OF TWO MASTERS

By CARLO GOLDONI

Translated by EDWARD J. DENT

Clarice, knowing Federigo Rasponi, to whom she was betrothed has been killed, has accepted Silvio, whom she loves. Beatrice Rasponi, disguised as her dead brother, comes to Venice seeking Florindo, whom she loves, but who is thought to have killed her brother in a duel.

SCENE—*A room in the house of Pantalone, a Venetian merchant, and father to Clarice.*

TIME—*Eighteenth century.*

BEATRICE. Signora Clarice, I beg you . . .

CLARICE. Stand away, and do not dare to importune me.

BEATRICE. So severe with him who is your destined husband?

CLARICE. They may drag me by force to the altar, but you will have only my hand, never my heart.

BEATRICE. You disdain me, but I hope to appease you.

CLARICE. I shall abhor you to all eternity.

BEATRICE. But if you knew me, you would not say so.

CLARICE. I know you well enough as the destroyer of my happiness.

BEATRICE. But I can find a way to comfort you.

CLARICE. You deceive yourself; there is no-one who can comfort me but Silvio.

BEATRICE. 'Tis true, I cannot give you the same comfort as your Silvio might, but I can at least contribute to your happiness.

CLARICE. I think it is quite enough, sir, that although I speak to you as harshly as I can, you should continue to torture me.

BEATRICE (*aside*) Poor girl! I can't bear to see her suffer.

CLARICE (*aside*) I'm so angry, I don't care how rude I am.

BEATRICE. Signora Clarice, I have a secret to tell you.

CLARICE. I make no promise to keep it; you had better not tell it me.

BEATRICE. Your severity deprives me of the means to make you happy.

CLARICE. You can never make me anything but miserable.

BEATRICE. You are wrong, and to convince you I will speak plainly. You have no desire for me, I have no use for you. You have promised your hand to another, I to another have already pledged my heart.

CLARICE. Oh! Now you begin to please me.

BEATRICE. Did I not tell you that I knew how to comfort you?

CLARICE. Ah, I feared you would deceive me.

BEATRICE. Nay, madam, I speak in all sincerity; and if you promise me that discretion which you refused me just now, I will confide to you a secret, which will ensure your peace of mind.

CLARICE. I vow I will observe the strictest silence.

BEATRICE. I am not Federigo Rasponi, but his sister Beatrice.

CLARICE. What! I am amazed. You a woman?

BEATRICE. I am indeed. Imagine my feelings when I claimed you as my bride!

CLARICE. And what news have you of your brother?

BEATRICE. He died indeed by the sword. A lover of mine was thought to have killed him, and 'tis he whom I am seeking now in these clothes. I beseech you by all the holy laws of friendship and of love not to betray me.

CLARICE. Won't you let me tell Silvio?

BEATRICE. No; on the contrary I forbid you absolutely.

CLARICE. Well, I will say nothing.

BEATRICE. Remember I count upon you.

CLARICE. You have my promise. I will be silent.

BEATRICE. Now, I hope, you will treat me more kindly.

CLARICE. I will be your friend indeed; and if I can be of service to you, dispose of me.

BEATRICE. I too swear eternal friendship to you. Give me your hand.

CLARICE. I don't quite like to . . .

BEATRICE. Are you afraid I am not a woman after all? I will give you proof positive.

CLARICE. It all seems just like a dream.

BEATRICE. Yes. 'Tis a strange business.

CLARICE. 'Tis indeed fantastic.

BEATRICE. Come, I must be going. Let us embrace in sign of honest friendship and loyalty.

CLARICE. There! I doubt you no longer.

THE SHOEMAKER'S HOLIDAY

by THOMAS DEKKER

Rose, daughter of the Lord Mayor of London, has fallen in love with Rowland Lacy, nephew of the rich Earl of Lincoln. The match is not approved; Rose has been sent away with her maid, Sibyl, and plans are being made to send Lacy abroad.

SCENE—*A garden at Old Ford.*
TIME—*1599.*

ROSE.   Here sit thou down upon this flowery bank,
And make a garland for thy Lacy's head.
These pinks, these roses and these violets,
These blushing gillyflowers, these marigolds,
The fair embroidery of his coronet,
Carry not half such beauty in their cheeks
As the sweet countenance of my Lacy doth.
O my most unkind father! O my stars,
Why lowered you so at my nativity,
To make me love, yet live robbed of my love?
Here as a thief am I imprisoned
For my dear Lacy's sake within these walls
Which by my father's cost were builded up
For better purposes; here must I languish
For him that doth as much lament I know,
Mine absence, as for him I pine in woe.

(*Enter* SYBIL, *her maid*)

SYBIL. Good morrow, young mistress. I am sure you make that garland for me; against I shall be Lady of the Harvest.

ROSE. Sybil, what news at London?

SYBIL. None but good; my lord mayor, your father, and Master Philpot, your uncle, and Master Scot, your cousin, and Mistress Frigbottom by Doctors' Commons, do all, by my troth, send you most hearty commendations.

ROSE. Did Lacy send kind greetings to his love?

SYBIL. O yes, out of cry, by my troth, I scant knew him; here a' wore a scarf; and here a scarf, here a bunch of feathers, and here precious stones and jewels, and a pair of garters,—O, monstrous! like one of our yellow silk curtains at home here in Old Ford House, here in Master Bellymount's chamber. I stood at our door in Cornhill, looked at him, he at me indeed, spake to him, but he not to me, not a word; marry-go-up, thought I with a wanion! He passed by me as proud—marry foh! are you grown humorous, thought I; and so shut the door and in I came.

ROSE.   O Sybil, how dost thou my Lacy wrong!
My Rowland is as gentle as a lamb,
No dove was ever half so mild as he.

SYBIL. Mild? yea, as a bushel of stamped crabs. He looked upon me as sour as verjuice. Go thy ways, thought I; thou mayst be much in my gaskins but nothing in my netherstocks. This is your fault, mistress, to love him that loves not you; he thinks scorn to do as he's done to; but if I were as you, I'd cry: "Go by, Jeronimo, go by."

I'd set my old debts against my new driblets,
And the hare's foot against the goose giblets,
For if ever I sigh, when sleep I should take,
Pray God I may lose my maidenhead when I wake!

ROSE. Will my love leave me then and go to France?

SYBIL. I know not that. But I am sure I see him stalk before the soldiers. By my troth, he is a proper man; but he is proper that proper doth. Let him go snick up, young mistress.

ROSE.   Get thee to London, and learn perfectly,
Whether my Lacy go to France or no.
Do this, and I will give thee for thy pains
My cambric apron and my Romish gloves,
My purple stockings and a stomacher.
Say, wilt thou do this, Sybil, for my sake?

SYBIL. Will I quoth: "At whose suit? By my troth, yes, I'll go. A cambric apron, gloves, a pair of purple stockings, and a stomacher! I'll sweat in purple, mistress, for you; I'll take anything that comes a God's name. O rich! a cambric apron! Faith, then have at up tails all. I'll go jiggy-joggy to London, and be here in a trice, young mistress.

(SYBIL *exits*)

ROSE.   Do so, good Sybil. Meantime wretched I
Will sit and sigh for his lost company.

---

out of cry . . . beyond measure.
wanion . . . vengeance.
stamped crabs . . . crushed crab apples
Go by, Jeronimo. . . . "Hieronimo, beware". A line from Kyd's "The Spanish Tragedy".
snick up . . . be hanged.
have at 'up tails all . . . start with alacrity.

SIWAN

By Saunders Lewis

Translated by Emyr Humphreys

Llywelyn the Great has chained and imprisoned his wife, Siwan, since discovering that she has a lover, Gwilym de Breos. Only her maid, Alis, is permitted to visit her.

SCENE—*A room in the tower, Llywelyn's castle.*
TIME—*6 a.m., 3rd May 1230.*

ALIS.   Madame, are you awake?
SIWAN.   I have not slept.
ALIS.   Not at all? Not for two nights, madame?
SIWAN.   I am not used to being shackled to my bed.
         The irons are heavy, Alis, Welsh style in bracelets.
         Feel the weight, feel the weight of a Prince's anger.
ALIS (*as Siwan drags the chains along the floor*)
         Of his disappointment, madame;—
         His disappointment much more than his displeasure.
         Does it hurt very much?
SIWAN.   It hurts my pride so much, I don't feel
         The pain in my leg.
         I have sent men to prison;
         I never imagined the shame of feet in chains.
ALIS.   The Prince has said the chain shall be kept on only for
           today.
SIWAN.   Why today and not after today?
         Can today change my condition?
ALIS (*to avoid giving a direct answer*)
         Let me ease your condition, madame.
         I have some wine here.
SIWAN.   Did he send you here?
ALIS.   To serve you and do your bidding.
         I can come and go: bring you things; the porter knows.
SIWAN.   The porter is a mute. All day yesterday I saw no-one
         But that dumb man at the door.
ALIS.   A dumb porter can't spread gossip.
SIWAN.   Or carry messages from the prison.
         That's why he was chosen.
         Well, why should I have a maid-in-waiting now to carry
           messages?

122

My condition must change?
ALIS. Will you take some wine?
SIWAN. This wine is sour; it suits my thirst. . . .
The third of May, is it?
ALIS. Yes, the third, my lady.
SIWAN. Two days and two nights in the cell's silence;
So long ago it was the first of May.
Alis, did you ever sleep alone in a chamber?
ALIS. Oh, no, madame. I'm not a Princess.
I have slept in my place, among the other women on the
floor.
SIWAN. The solitude of a prison is different, and somehow amaz-
ing,
A hermit's world, where the tongue has no function.
ALIS. You were never very talkative, madame.
SIWAN. I know. Having nothing to say
In the midst of revelling has often been a burden to me.
But here it is not my own silence I have to bear—
Here it is the dumb walls, the dumb man at the door, the
uncertainty
That build the silence.
In daylight, yesterday, I heard nothing here
But my own heart beating hour by hour.
What hour of morning is it now, Alis?
ALIS. The sixth hour, madame.
SIWAN. Add those to twenty-four, and another twenty-four,
I have been here almost sixty hours.
Once I heard a learned teacher, an Augustinian say
That in eternity Time does not exist. I hope he's right;
Staring out the glare in the eye of time is the start of
madness.
In time there is time for everything—so there is no
security,
Time is always a threat, like that hammering that began
before dawn.
ALIS. You have not slept, madame, not for three days.
Or touched the food sent to you.
No wonder you are nervous and distraught.
SIWAN. Why were you sent to me?
ALIS. To serve you and be at your command.
SIWAN. The Prince himself sent you?
ALIS. Yes, my lady, the Prince himself.
Otherwise the guard would not have let me pass.
SIWAN. I suspect it. He said you could come and go for me
And do my bidding. Can you carry messages
From one prison to another?
ALIS. I couldn't say, my lady. He didn't mention that.
SIWAN. I have no other message. (*Pause*)

	What is that endless hammering on the lawn?
ALIS.	Something the soldiers are doing. Some exercise I expect.
SIWAN.	Didn't you see what it was on your way here?
ALIS.	I didn't notice. I was told to hurry.
	Is the wine warming, madame?
SIWAN.	Go to the window and look: this chain ties me to the wall
	Like a bear to a post. You are not a bitch to bait me, girl.
	What are they putting up? Stand by the window and tell
	me.
ALIS.	They are soldiers, madame.
SIWAN.	Soldiers. I know they are soldiers. You've said so already.
	I never saw soldiers before doing carpentry on the castle
	lawn.
	Snowdonia can't go to war because of this:
	It's no preparation for war. Tell me
	What are they building?
ALIS.	It's not possible to see between these narrow bars.
SIWAN.	Don't lie, girl. I know how much you can see.
	I've stared through that window myself before today.
	What are they doing? Answer me, girl.
ALIS.	Oh, please, my lady, don't ask me that again.
	On my knees I beg you, allow me to go from here.
SIWAN.	My poor child, what is it? Don't tremble and cry;
	Tell me quietly what are they making on the lawn?
ALIS.	A gibbet, madame, a gallows.
SIWAN.	A gallows? (*She laughs incredulously*)
	Good for you, Llywelyn. So that's my punishment?
	My little Alis, don't cry, about that.
ALIS.	Not for you, madame, not for you.
SIWAN.	What?
ALIS.	A gallows for Gwilym de Breos.

SPRING 1600

By EMLYN WILLIAMS

Ann Byrd escapes from impending marriage and disguised as a boy actor, named Jack Beeston, joins the Lord Chamberlain's Players, headed by the actor Richard Burbage, with whom she falls in love. Lady Coperario, the beautiful, sophisticated courtesan, at first intrigued by Jack's acting, becomes fascinated by the maturer actor, Richard, who hopes through her, to secure the patronage of the Duke of Lennox for his new Globe Theatre.

SCENE—*Richard Burbage's bedchamber, in his house in Shoreditch, London.*
TIME—*1600.*

(*Far away, the strumming of a lute, which gradually approaches;* ANN *listens, her face softening. She looks upstairs, looks down at the bracelet she is holding, slips it on, rises and goes to her locker; she takes out two plaits of her own hair, a broken piece of mirror, and from the heap on the basket, a woman's dress for the play. She ties the plaits round her head, drapes the dress round her, and studies herself in the mirror, to the cadence of the music. The music dies away.*)

LADY COPERARIO *enters, she comes down and sees* ANN (*who has not heard her enter*) *bend gracefully before the mirror, arranging her hair*)

LADY COPERARIO (*amused*) Buona sera, madam. (*As* ANN *starts*) Music, and moonlight in spring . . . what more could delight a woman's heart?

(ANN *hastily throws her dress and the plaits of hair on to the settle, and faces her, square and awkward*)

ANN. Jack Beeston, at your service.
LADY COPERARIO. Beeston? The boy player?
ANN (*pulling off the bracelet*) I am he, my lady.

(LADY COPERARIO *comes down, puzzled, and gives a long look*)

LADY COPERARIO. Unfold your arms, Jack Beeston, and join your knees; for you are no playing boy, or any other sort of boy either.

(*As* ANN *stands, mute and defiant*)

Are you a witch in danger of burning, or a harlot who's murdered her man in his sleep?
ANN. I was brought to London by one of the players, I was safe with him. . . .

125

LADY COPERARIO (*her anger rising*) *You* safe with *him!* The question is, was he safe with you? You innocent little trull, chasing up and down the country after the men, and ending up, perdio, in the bedchamber of Richard Burbage! (*Furiously*) This is a pretty stone I have turned over by accident—and what do I find underneath, per grazia di . . .

ANN. Your Italian oaths are wasted on me . . .

LADY COPERARIO. Would you prefer I pour out good Billingsgate abuse, that you would better understand?

ANN. I only know it would pour out more natural.

LADY COPERARIO. You pinch-penny, you trollop . . .

ANN. That's better . . .

LADY COPERARIO. A green boy-actor, learning his trade—and plying it, too, I'll swear, with the great player! I'll have you driven down Fleet Street, my girl, with a brass basin beating before you, to tell the city of your shame. That I should live to fight a London mopsy for the favours of a man . . .

ANN. Fight? And what are *my* weapons, against yours, in the tiltyard of passion? Have *I* pearls from the deep seas of love, strung round my neck? Have *I* blood-red rings of love in my ears, and all the warm scents of love deep in my hair?

LADY COPERARIO (*perplexed*) But when you turn back into a woman, all these things may again be yours—what talk is this . . .

ANN. Yes, when I turn back into a woman! Shall I tell you how the proud Miss Byrd of Ongar has made herself into the prize fool of Cheapside? (*Walking up and down, the truth pouring out at last*) She would catch no more butterflies and learn no more Latin; but fiddled her nose at her bridegroom and turned overnight into a man; and wallowed in mud and rode crossways on a horse, and learnt to swear and drink beer . . . But it was worth it, for she curtsied to nobody! I stood one morning, my feet astride the city wall over Moorgate, and I laughed aloud to the sky, because I wore a doublet and hose . . . because I was free!

LADY COPERARIO. And now?

ANN. Now . . . (*Sitting, on the chest*) The sky is not free, but empty. For as I stood, my boots apart, so fine and manly, an arrow was shot . . . and struck me. All this night, while you and he will be together, I am the one that must lie in tears, dejected . . . a woman!

LADY COPERARIO. While he and I will be together? Tonight?

ANN. I myself took the message. (*She holds out the bracelet*)

(LADY COPERARIO *crosses to her, and studies it*)

LADY COPERARIO (*gently*) What are your thoughts of him?

ANN. I have no other. They are of his smiles and his curses, his tenderness and his raging. . . . And you have come . . . (*Her voice breaks*)

(*A pause*)

LADY COPERARIO (*thoughtfully*) Little Miss Byrd . . . that was no messenger of mine. Master Burbage does not visit me tonight.

ANN. Then who . . .

LADY COPERARIO. I could give you six names, where you might find the lady of his—current choice. (*Throwing the bracelet into a corner of the throne*) In the chronology of *his* heart, a week is a long time indeed. And rather than love Richard Burbage, it will pay you to nurse a passion for the water that slips under London Bridge to a sea that you know nothing of.

(*Outside the front door the blackamoor strums lazily on the lute*)

ANN. Then why have you come?

LADY COPERARIO. Why? (*Shrugging her shoulders*) Out of curiosity —anger—weakness . . .

ANN. And out of—love?

LADY COPERARIO (*after a pause*) I cannot enjoy it. (*Sitting on the throne*) I am a woman that has turned the desires of men into a shining life for myself; and to me humble bread is bitter bread indeed. And yet tonight, in my outlandish barge, my blackamoor playing music . . . I am here. Keep your secret from Richard Burbage.

ANN (*as the lute dies away*) Does love turn so soon to malice?

LADY COPERARIO. So soon? . . . (*Lightly*) It is a perfume, my child, that one night you hold to your face, for the scent is so fine it will be lost unless it be caught so . . . And in the morning . . .

ANN. In the morning?

LADY COPERARIO. There is a difference; so crafty that you are nearly deceived into smiling again, with the freshness of that heavenly odour . . . But the difference is there; the scent is dulled with a breath no stronger than a sigh, and you wake, to find that love . . . has turned sour.

A TASTE OF HONEY

By Shelagh Delaney

Helen, a coarse, tarty, but basically warm-hearted woman, and sixteen-year-old Jo, her moody, intelligent daughter, always on the move, are in depressing new digs.

Scene—*A comfortless flat in Manchester.*
Time—*The present.*

Helen. Jo! Jo! Come on. Be sharp now.

(Jo *comes on in her pyjamas. She has a heavy cold*)

For God's sake give me a hand. I'll never be ready. What time is it? Have a look at the church clock.

Jo. A quarter past eleven, and the sun's coming out.

Helen. Oh! Well, happy the bride the sun shines on.

Jo. Yeah, and happy the corpse the rain rains on. You're not getting married in a church, are you?

Helen. Why, are you coming to throw bricks at us? Of course not. Do I look all right? Pass me my fur. Oh! My fur! Do you like it?

Jo. I bet somebody's missing their cat.

Helen. It's a wedding present from that young man of mine. He spends his money like water, you know, penny wise, pound foolish. Oh! I am excited. I feel twenty-one all over again. Oh! You would have to catch a cold on my wedding day. I was going to ask you to be my bridesmaid too.

Jo. Don't talk daft.

Helen. Where did you put my shoes? Did you clean 'em? Oh! They're on my feet. Don't stand there sniffing, Jo. Use a handkerchief.

Jo. I haven't got one.

Helen. Use this, then. What's the matter with you? What are you trying to hide?

Jo. Nothing.

Helen. Don't try to kid me. What is it? Come on, let's see.

Jo. It's nothing. Let go of me. You're hurting.

Helen. What's this?

Jo. A ring.

Helen. I can see it's a ring. Who give it to you?

Jo. A friend of mine.

Helen. Who? Come on. Tell me.

Jo. You're hurting me.

(HELEN *breaks the cord and gets the ring*)

HELEN. You should have sewn some buttons on your pyjamas if you didn't want me to see. Who give it you?

Jo. My boy friend. He asked me to marry him.

HELEN. Well, you silly little bitch. You mean that lad you've been knocking about with while we've been away?

Jo. Yes.

HELEN. I could choke you.

Jo. You've already had a damn good try.

HELEN. You haven't known him five minutes. Has he really asked you to marry him?

Jo. Yes.

HELEN. Well, thank God for the divorce courts! I suppose just because I'm getting married you think you should.

Jo. Have you got the monopoly?

HELEN. You stupid little devil! What sort of a wife do you think you'd make? You're useless. It takes you all your time to look after yourself. I suppose you think you're in love. Anybody can fall in love, do you know that? But what do you know about the rest of it?

Jo. Ask yourself.

HELEN. You know where that ring should be? In the ashcan with everything else. Oh! I could kill her, I could really.

Jo. You don't have to knock me about. I hope you suffer for it.

HELEN. I've done my share of suffering if I never do any more. Oh, Jo, you're only a kid. Why don't you learn from my mistakes? It takes half your life to learn from your own.

Jo. You leave me alone. Can I have my ring back, please?

HELEN. What a thing to happen just when I'm going to enjoy myself for a change.

Jo. Nobody's stopping you.

HELEN. Yes, and soon as my back's turned you'll be off with this sailor boy and ruin yourself for good.

Jo. I'm already ruined.

HELEN. Yes, it's just the sort of thing you'd do. You make me sick.

Jo. You've no need to worry, Helen. He's gone away. He may be back in six months, but there again, he may . . .

HELEN. Look, you're only young. Enjoy your life. Don't get trapped. Marriage can be hell for a kid.

Jo. Can I have your hanky back?

HELEN. Where did you put it?

Jo. This is your fault too.

HELEN. Everything's my fault. Show me your tongue.

Jo. Breathing your 'flu bugs all over me.

HELEN. Yes, and your neck's red where I pulled that string.

Jo. Will you get me a drink of water, Helen?

HELEN. No, have a dose of this. (*Offering whisky*) It'll do you more good. I might as well have one myself while I'm at it, mightn't I?

Jo. You've emptied more bottles down your throat in the last few weeks than I would have thought possible. If you don't watch it, you'll end up an old down-and-out boozer knocking back the meths.

HELEN. It'll never come to that. The devil looks after his own, they say.

Jo. He certainly takes good care of you. You look marvellous, considering.

HELEN. Considering what?

Jo. The wear and tear on your soul.

HELEN. Oh well, that'll have increased its market value, won't it?

Jo. Old Nick'll get you in the end.

HELEN. Thank God for that! Heaven must be the hell of a place. Nothing but repentant sinners up there, isn't it? All the pimps, prostitutes and politicians in creation trying to cash in on eternity and their little tin god. Where's my hat?

Jo. Where's your husband?

HELEN. Probably drunk with his pals somewhere. He was going down to the house this morning to let some air in. Have you seen a picture of the house? Yes, you have. Do you like it? (*She peers and primps into the mirror*)

Jo. It's all right if you like that sort of thing, and I don't.

HELEN. I'll like it in a few years, when it isn't so new and clean. At the moment it's like my face, unblemished! Oh look at that, every line tells a dirty story, hey?

Jo. Will you tell me something before you go?

HELEN. Oh! You can read all about that in books.

Jo. What was my father like?

(HELEN *turns away*)

HELEN. Who?

Jo. You heard! My father! What was he like?

HELEN. Oh! Him.

Jo. Well, was he so horrible that you can't even tell me about him?

HELEN. He wasn't horrible. He was just a bit stupid, you know. Not very bright.

Jo. Be serious, Helen.

HELEN. I am serious.

Jo. Are you trying to tell me he was an idiot?

HELEN. He wasn't an idiot, he was just a bit—retarded.

Jo. You liar!

HELEN. All right, I'm a liar.

Jo. Look at me.

HELEN. Well, am I?

Jo. No.

Helen. Well, now you know.

Jo. How could you give me a father like that?

Helen. I didn't do it on purpose. How was I to know you'd materialize out of a little love affair that lasted five minutes?

Jo. You never think. That's your trouble.

Helen. I know.

Jo. Was he like a . . . a real idiot?

Helen. I've told you once. He was nice though, you know, a nice little feller!

Jo. Where is he now, locked up?

Helen. No, he's dead.

Jo. Why?

Helen. Why? Well, I mean, death's something that comes to us all, and when it does come you haven't usually got time to ask why.

Jo. It's hereditary, isn't it?

Helen. What?

Jo. Madness.

Helen. Sometimes.

Jo. Am I mad?

Helen. Decide for yourself. Oh, Jo, don't be silly. Of course you're not daft. Not more so than anybody else.

Jo. Why did you have to tell me that story? Couldn't you have made something up?

Helen. You asked for the truth and you got it for once. Now be satisfied.

Jo. How could you go with a half-wit!

Helen. He had strange eyes. You've got 'em. Everybody used to laugh at him. Go on, I'll tell you some other time.

Jo. Tell me now!

Helen. Mind my scent!

Jo. Please tell me. I want to understand.

Helen. Do you think I understand? For one night, actually it was the afternoon, I loved him. It was the first time I'd ever really been with a man . . .

Jo. You were married.

Helen. I was married to a Puritan—do you know what I mean?

Jo. I think so.

Helen. And when I met your father I was as pure and unsullied as I fondly, and perhaps mistakenly, imagine you to be. It was the first time and though you can enjoy the second, the third, even the fourth time, there's no time like the first, it's always there. I'm off now. I've got to go and find my husband. Now don't sit here sulking all day.

Jo. I was thinking.

Helen. Well, don't think. It doesn't do you any good. I'll see you when the honeymoon's over. Come on, give us a kiss. You may as well. It's a long time since you kissed me.

Jo. Keep it for him.

HELEN. I don't suppose you're sorry to see me go.

Jo. I'm not sorry and I'm not glad.

HELEN. You don't know what you do want.

Jo. Yes, I do. I've always known what I want.

HELEN. And when it comes your way will you recognize it?

Jo. Good luck, Helen.

HELEN. I'll be seeing you. Hey! If he doesn't show up I'll be back.

Jo. Good luck, Helen.

Exit HELEN. *"Here comes the Bride" on the cornet.*

CURTAIN

TRELAWNY OF THE "WELLS"

By Sir Arthur Wing Pinero

Rose Trelawny, the beautiful, nineteen-year-old popular actress of the "Wells" tells her friend, Imogen Parrot, a pretty, light-hearted actress of about twenty-seven, why she is leaving the stage to marry into the aristocracy.

SCENE—*The sitting-room of a respectable lodging-house.*
Time—1898.

ROSE (*meeting Imogen* C) Dear Imogen!

IMOGEN (*kissing her*) Rose dear!

ROSE. I've so much to say to you. Imogen, the brilliant hits you've made! How lucky you have been!

IMOGEN. *My* luck! What about *yours?*

ROSE (*leaning back in the chair, right hand on table*) Yes, isn't this a wonderful stroke of fortune for me! Fate, Jenny! that's what it is— Fate! (*Extending her left hand to front*) Fate ordains that I shall be a well-to-do fashionable lady, instead of a popular but toiling actress. Mother often used to stare into my face, when I was little, and whisper, "Rosie, I wonder what is to be your—fate." (*She raises her head and looks up to front*) Poor mother! I hope she *sees.*

IMOGEN.. Your Arthur seems nice.

ROSE. Oh, he's a dear. Very young, of course—not much more than a year older than me—than I. But he'll grow manly in time, and have moustaches, and whiskers out to here, he says.

IMOGEN. How did you . . . ?

ROSE. He saw me act Blanche in *The Pedlar of Marseilles,* and fell in love.

IMOGEN. Do you prefer Blanche . . . ?

ROSE. To Celestine? Oh, yes. You see, I got leave to introduce a song—(*looking towards* R) where Blanche is waiting for Raphael on the bridge.

(GADD *comes down to the table to pick a flower from the dish, and puts it in his buttonhole*)

(*Singing, dramatically but in low tones*) "Ever of thee I'm fondly dreaming . . ."

IMOGEN. I know . . .

(*They sing together*)

ROSE
IMOGEN } "Thy gentle voice my spirit can cheer."

ROSE. It was singing that song that sealed my destiny, Arthur declares. At any rate, the next thing was he began sending bouquets (*gesture of arm to* R) and coming to the stage-door. (*Gesture of arm to* L) Of course, I never spoke to him, never glanced at him. (*Hands clasped on lap*) Poor mother brought me up in that way, not to speak to anybody, nor look.

IMOGEN. Quite right.

ROSE (*her head up*) I do hope she sees.

IMOGEN. And then . . . ?

ROSE. Then Arthur managed to get acquainted with the Telfers, and Mrs Telfer presented him to me. Mrs Telfer has kept an eye on me all through. Not that it was necessary, brought up as I was—but she's a kind old soul.

IMOGEN. And now you're going to live with his people for a time, aren't you?

ROSE. Yes—on approval.

(AVONIA *gets* R *of the table*)

IMOGEN. Ha, ha, ha! you don't mean that!

ROSE. Well, in a way—just to reassure them, as they put it. The Gowers have such odd ideas about theatres, and actors and actresses.

IMOGEN. Do you think you'll like the arrangement?

ROSE. It'll only be for a little while. I fancy they're prepared to take to me, especially Miss Trafalgar Gower . . .

IMOGEN. Trafalgar!

ROSE. Sir William's sister; she was born Trafalgar year, and christened after it . . .

IMOGEN (R, *cheerfully*) Well, God bless you, my dear. I'm afraid *I* couldn't give up the stage though, not for all the Arthurs . . .

ROSE (L *of Imogen*) Ah, your mother wasn't an actress.

IMOGEN. No.

ROSE. Mine was, and I remember her saying to me once, "Rose, if ever you have the chance, get out of it."

IMOGEN. The Profession?

ROSE. Yes. "Get out of it"; Mother said, "if ever a good man comes along, and offers to marry you and to take you off the stage, seize the chance—get out of it."

IMOGEN. Your mother was never popular, was she?

ROSE. Yes, indeed she was, most popular—till she grew oldish and lost her looks.

IMOGEN. Oh, *that's* what she meant then?

ROSE. Yes, that's what she meant.

(ABLETT *picks up his glove*)

IMOGEN (*shivering*) Oh, lor', doesn't it make one feel depressed! (*She looks at the table*)

ROSE. Poor Mother! Well, I hope she sees.

UNCLE VANYA

by Anton Chekhov

Translated by Elisaveta Fen

Both seventeen-year-old Sonya, gentle, charming, but not beautiful, and Yeliena, her father's attractive, intelligent twenty-seven-year-old second wife, are attracted to the doctor, Astrov.

SCENE—*A dining-room.*
TIME—*1897.*

SONYA (*alone*) He didn't say anything to me . . . his soul and his heart are still hidden from me, so why do I feel so happy? (*She laughs with happiness*) I told him: you have poise and nobility of mind and such a soft voice. . . . Did it sound out of place? His voice vibrates and caresses. . . . I can almost feel it in the air now. But when I said that to him about a younger sister he didn't understand. . . . Oh, how dreadful it is that I'm not good-looking! How dreadful! I know I'm plain, I know, I know! . . . Last Sunday as people were coming out of church I heard them talking about me and a woman said, "She's kind and generous, but what a pity she's so plain. . . ." So plain. . . .

(*Enter* YELIENA)

YELIENA (*opening the window*) The storm's over. What lovely fresh air! (*A pause*) Where's the doctor?
SONYA. He's gone.
YELIENA (*after a pause*) Sophie!
SONYA. What?
YELIENA. How long are you going to go on being sulky with me? We haven't done each other any harm . . . so why should we behave like enemies? Come, do let us stop it.
SONYA. I wanted to myself. . . . (*She embraces her*) Yes, don't let us be cross any more.
YELIENA. That's fine. (*Both are moved*)
SONYA. Has Papa gone to bed?
YELIENA. No, he's sitting in the drawing-room. . . . We don't speak to each other for weeks on end, but Heaven alone knows why. . . . (*She sees the open sideboard*) What's this?
SONYA. Mihail Lvovich has been having supper.
YELIENA. There's wine, too. . . . Let's drink to our friendship.
SONYA. Yes, let's.

YELIENA. Out of the same glass. (*She fills it*) It's better like that. Now we are real friends.

SONYA. Friends. (*They drink, then kiss one another*) I've been wanting to make it up for ever so long, but I felt so ashamed somehow. . . . (*She cries*)

YELIENA. But why are you crying?

SONYA. Never mind . . . there's no reason.

YELIENA. Come, there, there. . . . (*She cries*) I'm a queer creature —I've started crying too. (*A pause*) You're cross with me because you think I married your father for ulterior motives. . . . If you are impressed by oaths, I'll vow to you that I married him for love. I was attracted by him as a learned man, a celebrity. . . . It wasn't real love, it was all artificial, but you see, at that time it seemed real to me. I'm not to blame. But from the day of our marriage you've been punishing me with those shrewd suspicious eyes of yours.

SONYA. Come, peace, peace, let's forget about it!

YELIENA. You mustn't look at people like that—it doesn't suit you. You should believe everyone—or else you just can't live.

(*A pause*)

SONYA. Tell me, honestly, as a friend. . . . Are you happy?

YELIENA. No.

SONYA. I knew that. One more question. Tell me frankly . . . wouldn't you have liked your husband to be young?

YELIENA. What a little girl you are still! Of course I should. (*She laughs*) Well, ask me something else, do! . . .

SONYA. Do you like the doctor?

YELIENA. Yes, very much.

SONYA (*laughing*) Have I got a stupid face? . . . Yes? He's gone, but I can still hear his voice and his footsteps, and when I glance at the dark window I can see his face in it. . . . Do let me tell you about it. . . . But I mustn't speak so loudly, I feel ashamed. Come to my room, we'll talk there. Do I seem stupid to you? Own up. . . . Tell me something about him.

YELIENA. Well, what shall I tell you?

SONYA. He's so clever. . . . He knows how to do things, he can do anything. . . . He treats the sick, and he plants forests too. . . .

YELIENA. It isn't a question of forests or medicines. . . . My dear, don't you understand? . . . He's got talent! . . . And do you know what that means? Courage, freedom of mind, breadth of outlook. . . . He plants a tree and wonders what will come of it in a thousand years' time, and speculates on the future of mankind. Such people are rare and we must love them. . . . He drinks, sometimes he seems a little coarse—but what does it matter? A talented man can't stay free from blemishes in Russia. Just think what sort of life this doctor leads! Impassable mud on the roads, frost, snow-storms, vast distances, crude, primitive people, poverty and disease all around him —it's hard for a man who works and struggles day after day in such surroundings to keep pure and sober till he's forty. . . . (*She kisses her*) I wish you happiness with all my heart, you deserve it. . . . (*She gets up*) As for me, I'm just a tiresome person of no importance. In my music studies, in my home life in my husband's house, in all my romantic affairs—in fact in everything I've just been a person of no importance. Really, Sonya, when you come to think of it. I'm a very, very, unfortunate woman. (*She walks about in agitation*) There's no happiness for me on this earth. None! Why do you laugh?

SONYA (*laughing, hiding her face*) I am so happy . . . so happy! . . .

YELIENA. I should like to play something. . . . I should like to play something now.

SONYA. Do play! (*Embracing her*) I can't sleep. . . . Do play!

YELIENA. In a minute. Your father isn't asleep. When he's unwell, music irritates him. Go and ask him. If he doesn't mind, I'll play. Go.

SONYA. I'm going.

(SONYA *exits*)

YELIENA. It's a long time since I played the piano. I shall play and cry . . . cry like a foolish girl. . . .

SONYA (*returning*) We mustn't.

THE YOUNG ELIZABETH

By Jennette Dowling and Francis Letton

Princess Elizabeth, daughter of the late Henry VIII is living with her step-mother Queen Katherine, now married to Thomas Seymour. Elizabeth, gay, young and high-spirited, cannot accept the beliefs of her stepsister, the hard, relentless Mary Tudor.

SCENE—*The upstairs living-room in Katherine Parr's house, Chelsea.*
TIME—*1547.*

ELIZABETH (*as she enters*) Mary! It's true! You're here! (*She runs to Mary and puts her arms around her*)

MARY. Bess! (*She kisses Elizabeth*)

ELIZABETH. How long have you been here and they told me not? Have you seen Tom? He thought you hated us, and now you're here to give him the lie in it.

MARY. Oh, my poor innocent babe! What have they done to you? Bess, Bess, come away with me.

ELIZABETH. What?

MARY. I have come to fetch you from this place.

ELIZABETH. But, Mary, I am happy here, and cared for well.

MARY. Bess, sit you down.

(ELIZABETH *crosses and sits* R *of the table*)

(*She crosses and sits* L *of the table*) We two must stand together against those who plot against us.

ELIZABETH. What plot's afoot? I shall give it to Kate and Tom and they will stop it.

MARY. No, no, the plot's his.

ELIZABETH. Sweet saints, are you ill?

MARY. Listen to me, and let my words sink into your mind. First—know you the duties of a Christian wife?

ELIZABETH. Why, surely.

MARY. Think you they tell her to deny her husband, and take unto herself a lover in another?

ELIZABETH. No.

MARY. Yet this is the very thing the Queen has done against our father.

ELIZABETH. Our father's dead, and she has married Tom.

MARY. Bess, what do you know of men?

ELIZABETH. As much, I am sure, as you.

MARY. Then you do fear them.

138

ELIZABETH. No, surely. I do think men the noblest of God's creatures, and women only fortunate in being necessary to them.

MARY (*rising and crossing to* L) So speaks Kate Parr through you.

ELIZABETH (*rising*) Mary, I pray you, rid you of this humour. I like it not, nor you when you are in it.

MARY (*crossing to* C) I did not come here to quarrel.

ELIZABETH (*crossing to* R *of Mary*) God help me, I did not mean to. I—I have the things you sent me. (*She displays her gown*) Look.

MARY. Do you like the gown?

ELIZABETH. Excellent well.

MARY. Have you all that you need?

ELIZABETH. All! Kate's like a mother to me.

MARY (*moving* L) Kate!

ELIZABETH. I love her.

MARY (*moving sharply to* L *of Elizabeth*) Bess! How can I open your eyes? How can I teach you to know what is right, and what is the dangerous road with pitfalls in it, for those who have not truth in their hearts? There's evil in this house.

ELIZABETH. If what is here is evil, then before God, I am evil too, for I am part of it and like it well.

MARY. Here speaks the devil in you I must fight; your mother's devil.

ELIZABETH. Mary—I warn you, speak not of my mother.

MARY. I must.

ELIZABETH. Grant me my mother and I'll grant you yours. Speak no more of them.

MARY. My mother was a saint. (*She weeps*)

ELIZABETH. And mine was not. And both are dead! Therefore, peace! Oh God, you're weeping. (*She moves up* L)

MARY (*crossing and sitting* R *of the table*) Ay, for shame, for shame.

ELIZABETH. Well, don't. Tears fidget me.

MARY. A sister's tears!

ELIZABETH. Yours in particular, for I have been wet with them too many times. Oh, Mary—dry your eyes. I love you, Mary. (*She crosses and stands above the table*) Why do you weep?

MARY. I know what goes on in this house; Tom Seymour coming to see you in your chamber, as though you had given him access. And you take pride in it.

ELIZABETH (*moving below the table and kneeling* R *of Mary*) I love him. Why should I not be proud?

MARY. Has he touched you?

ELIZABETH. Often. And kissed me, too. I like it. My father used to kiss me once, and I did like that, too. Is this a sin?

MARY. All flesh is sin, and tampering with fleshly temptations is the devil's trap. If you are ignorant of it, then let me teach you true.

ELIZABETH. I pray my virginity be freer of suspicion than to need teaching.

MARY. Bess, take care, you have a dangerous tongue.

ELIZABETH. More so than yours?

MARY. Mine speaks the truth.

ELIZABETH. And twists it till it dies and lies in its grave.

MARY. You are your mother's daughter.

ELIZABETH. And if you are yours, I wonder not that my poor father turned from her.

MARY. Think you I'll ever be ashamed of that?

ELIZABETH. Are you a woman?

MARY. I am a woman.

ELIZABETH. Good—then for the love of God . . .

MARY. I am a woman, such as my mother was, not such a one as yours.

ELIZABETH. Mary . . .

MARY. Who earned and kept the name all England gave her—*whore!*

ELIZABETH (*rising and pointing to the door* R) You fiend—you devil! Get you from this place, or by my mother's name, I'll tear you limb from limb.

(MARY *rises and crosses to the door* R)

My fingers itch. And they have left their mark before.

MARY. I will not stay in this place for fear of hell.

(MARY *exits* R)

ELIZABETH. Mary—Mary . . . (*She covers her face with her hands for a moment, then, near tears, flings herself into the chair* L *of the table*)

MADE AND PRINTED IN GREAT BRITAIN BY
LATIMER TREND & COMPANY LTD PLYMOUTH
MADE IN ENGLAND